Palgrave Studies in Institutions, Economics and Law

Law and Economics is an interdisciplinary field of research that has emerged in recent decades, with research output increasing dramatically and academic programmes in law and economics multiplying. Increasingly, legal cases have an economic dimension and economic matters depend on rules and regulations. Increasingly, economists have realized that "institutions matter" because they influence economic activities. Increasingly, too, economics is used to improve our understanding of how institutions and how legal systems work. This new Palgrave Pivot series studies the intersection between law and economics, and addresses the need for greater interaction between the two disciplines.

Elena D'Agostino

The Determinants of Tax Evasion

Combining External Incentives and Intrinsic Motivations

palgrave
macmillan

Elena D'Agostino
University of Messina
Messina, Italy

ISSN 2662-6535 ISSN 2662-6543 (electronic)
Palgrave Studies in Institutions, Economics and Law
ISBN 978-3-032-21896-4 ISBN 978-3-032-21897-1 (eBook)
https://doi.org/10.1007/978-3-032-21897-1

This Palgrave Macmillan imprint is published by the registered company Springer Nature Switzerland AG

The registered company address is: Gewerbestrasse 11, 6330 Cham, Switzerland

Preface

Tax evasion is not a deviation, but rather a signal. It does not occur in the margins of legality, but in the heart of the fiscal contract. It is not the exception to the rule, but the rule under stress.

In every society, tax evasion persists. It adapts, evolves, and resists. It survives governments and often outlives them. It is not a technical anomaly, but a structural condition. And yet, despite its resilience, tax evasion remains one of the most underestimated threats to institutional legitimacy, democratic trust, and fiscal sustainability.

This book does not claim to be the first, nor will it be the last, to address the phenomenon. The author is fully aware that no theory, no model, and no empirical strategy will ever provide the definitive cure. Tax evasion is not a disease that can be eradicated, but a chronic condition that must be managed. All states, regardless of their institutional strength, must learn to live with it. But living with evasion must not mean tolerating it. The challenge is to keep the pathology in remission, to prevent it from metastasizing into systemic distrust, fiscal collapse, or democratic erosion.

Accepting the inevitability of tax evasion is not a surrender, but a call to strategic realism. It is an invitation to rethink the fiscal state not as a machine of extraction, but as a space of negotiation, cooperation, and institutional credibility. It is also a recognition that compliance cannot be imposed, but must be earned.

The governance of tax compliance has oscillated between coercion and trust. On one side, the deterrence paradigm: audits, penalties, surveillance. On the other, approaches centered on civic duty, tax morale, institutional trust. For decades, mainstream economic models historically emphasized deterrence, treating taxpayers as rational agents responding to incentives. But reality has proven more complex. Many comply without fear, and many evade despite it.

This book argues that the future of tax compliance lies not in choosing between deterrence and trust, but in understanding their interaction. It proposes a multidimensional framework that integrates economic incentives with psychological dispositions, legal structures with social norms, and institutional design with political legitimacy. It also suggests that sustainable compliance emerges not from enforcement alone, but from the strategic alignment of incentives and values.

Throughout the book, tax compliance is interpreted through a dual institutional perspective in which both enforcement mechanisms and institutional legitimacy contribute to shaping taxpayers' behavior. The underlying idea is that deterrence alone may prove unstable when disconnected from perceptions of fairness and reciprocity, while voluntary cooperation may remain fragile in the absence of credible enforcement. Compliance is therefore approached as an institutional process shaped by expectations on public institutions, enforcement credibility, and the perceived quality of the fiscal exchange.

The central question guiding this volume is: How do external incentives and intrinsic motivations interact to shape tax compliance, and under what institutional conditions can this interaction produce stable, credible, and resilient fiscal systems?

To answer this question, the book develops a layered analytical structure. It draws on economic theory, behavioral science, legal analysis, and political economy, combining conceptual reflection with empirical evidence, and proposing a strategic model of compliance based on game theory. The aim is not only to explain tax behavior, but to offer normative guidance for policy design in an era of fiscal stress, digital transformation, and democratic fragility.

The structure of this book follows a progressive analytical trajectory, guiding the reader from conceptual reflection to strategic modeling through an interdisciplinary perspective. Each chapter develops and deepens the arguments introduced in the previous one, moving from the multidimensional interpretation of tax evasion to the strategic mechanisms underlying tax compliance. Rather than offering a fragmented collection of perspectives, the book advances an integrated view of tax evasion as an institutional and behavioral phenomenon shaped by social interaction.

The first chapter lays the foundation by challenging the conventional view of tax evasion as a purely economic or legal infraction. Instead, it presents evasion as a multidimensional challenge that cuts across disciplines and defies reductionist explanations. Drawing from economics, law, political science, sociology, and psychology, the chapter constructs a panoramic view of the phenomenon. It argues that tax evasion is not simply a failure of enforcement, but a reflection of deeper tensions within the fiscal contract. It is a mirror of how citizens perceive the state, how institutions communicate legitimacy, and how societies negotiate the boundaries between obligation and trust. What is new here is the integration of these disciplinary lenses into a unified interpretive approach, where evasion is treated not as deviance, but as a signal, an indicator of institutional fragility, civic disengagement, and normative ambiguity. The chapter introduces the idea that taxation is not only a technical instrument of revenue collection, but also a symbolic and relational practice, capable of generating meaning, identity, and resistance.

The second chapter develops the analytical core of the book by exploring the interaction between external incentives and intrinsic motivations. It revisits classical deterrence theory, rooted in the rational choice paradigm, and juxtaposes it with behavioral economics and psychological insights. The chapter does not merely summarize existing models but tries to synthesize them into a dynamic perspective that captures the complexity of taxpayer behavior. It introduces the concept of motivational postures, the slippery slope framework, and the crowding-out effect, showing how enforcement strategies can either reinforce or undermine voluntary compliance. What makes this chapter original is its refusal to treat compliance as a linear function of enforcement. Instead, it presents compliance as a contingent outcome, shaped by perceptions of fairness, institutional trust, civic duty, and social norms. The chapter discusses a taxonomy of taxpayer profiles and suggests that effective policy must be segmented, adaptive, and sensitive to the psychological architecture of motivation. It is here that the book begins to articulate its normative vision: that sustainable compliance cannot be achieved through coercion alone, but must be cultivated through institutional credibility, civic engagement, and cooperative norms.

The third chapter turns to the empirical challenge of measuring tax evasion. It begins with a paradox: how can we quantify a phenomenon that is, by definition, hidden? The chapter does not shy away from this difficulty but embraces it as a methodological and epistemological problem. It critically examines the concept of the tax gap, the limitations of audit-based extrapolation, and the biases inherent in macroeconomic models. The main idea is that measurement is not a neutral act, but a form of governance: what we choose to measure, and how we measure it, shapes our understanding of the problem and our response to it. The chapter introduces the idea of plausibility as an alternative to precision, suggesting that in the realm of evasion, approximation may be more honest than false exactitude. It also includes a comparative section that shows how different countries construct and interpret evasion, revealing the role of institutional capacity, legal definitions, and political narratives. The originality of this chapter lies in its epistemic reflexivity: it does not treat data as given, but as constructed, contested, and normatively charged.

The fourth and final chapter brings together the insights developed throughout the book into a stylized game-theoretic model of tax compliance. Using a strategic model, it conceptualizes the relationship between taxpayers and the state as an interaction shaped by enforcement effectiveness, public expenditure quality, transparency, and taxpayer expectations. The model identifies multiple equilibrium configurations, ranging from deterrence-based compliance to low-cooperation environments characterized by weak institutional credibility and persistent incentives toward evasion. It also highlights the role of monitoring and conditional cooperation, showing how taxpayers' ability to evaluate public expenditure quality may influence compliance decisions. Rather than mechanically reproducing real-world tax systems, the model offers a simplified strategic framework for interpreting heterogeneous institutional environments and for analyzing how different combinations of enforcement, institutional credibility, and public goods provision may shape fiscal behavior.

The book concludes with a reflection on the future of tax compliance, suggesting that the fiscal state must be reimagined not as a machine of extraction, but as a space of co-production. It calls for a shift from surveillance to cooperation, from punishment to participation, and from control to legitimacy. The final message is clear: tax compliance is not a transaction, but a relationship. And like all relationships, it requires care, reciprocity, and imagination.

Messina
June 2026

Elena D'Agostino

Contents

CHAPTER 1

Tax Evasion as a Multidimensional Challenge

Abstract This chapter provides a panoramic view of tax evasion through economic, political, sociological, legal, and psychological lenses. It critiques reductionist explanations and argues that evasion is embedded in institutional design, cultural norms, and perceptions of fairness. The economic perspective highlights incentive structures and welfare distortions, while the political lens frames evasion as a challenge to legitimacy and democratic consent. Sociological insights reveal how norms and identities shape compliance, and legal analysis underscores the ambiguity between evasion and avoidance. The psychological dimension introduces tax morale and the emotional cost of evasion, challenging the assumption that compliance is purely rational. By integrating these perspectives, the chapter constructs a unified interpretive framework to evaluate noncompliance within its sociopolitical context. It sets the stage for subsequent chapters by emphasizing the need for interdisciplinary strategies to address compliance.

Keywords Multidisciplinary analysis • Legal ambiguity • Social norms • Political legitimacy • Behavioral complexity

E. D'Agostino, *The Determinants of Tax Evasion*, Palgrave Studies in Institutions, Economics and Law,
https://doi.org/10.1007/978-3-032-21897-1_1

1.1 Introduction

Tax evasion is one of the most enduring paradoxes of modern governance. It is universally condemned yet persistently practiced.

Cross-country evidence suggests that the tax evasion continues to represent a significant challenge for many economies, while improvements in administrative performance are often associated with stronger tax collection capacity. It suggests that enforcement quality and institutional design are policy levers in their own right (Besley and Persson 2014).

In addition, international reforms have curtailed some forms of offshore evasion, yet domestic evasion and base erosion remain resilient, especially at the top of the wealth distribution. Compliance is therefore a moving target shaped by regulation and strategic adaptation.

Yet, despite technological advances, international coordination, and increasingly sophisticated enforcement, no country has eradicated it, not even those with high institutional quality and strong compliance cultures.

What has been said invites a deeper inquiry: if tax evasion is so clearly harmful, why does it remain so resilient?

A provocative answer may be stated upfront. In a world stripped of legal, moral, and social constraints, underreporting is often a rational free-riding response: the private gain from non-payment is immediate, while the costs are diluted across the tax-paying majority.

Taxation, however, is not merely a technical matter of revenue collection and, therefore, its persistence is not just a policy failure: above all, it is a signal of deeper tensions between state and society, between legality and legitimacy, and between individual rationality and collective responsibility.

For this reason, this chapter explores tax evasion through five disciplinary lenses, (economic, political, sociological, legal, and psychological), each offering distinct insights into its causes, consequences, and normative implications. By doing so, rather than previewing analytical models or behavioral frameworks, the chapter aims to frame the problem in its full complexity. It asks not only why individuals evade taxes, but what evasion reveals about the functioning of institutions, the legitimacy of fiscal systems, and the moral architecture of compliance.

This perspective is also consistent with approaches emphasizing the relational and legitimacy-based dimensions of taxation, according to which taxpayers respond not only to sanctions, but also to reciprocity and institutional credibility (Levi 1988; Feld and Frey 2007).

The following sections develop these perspectives through a multidisciplinary approach. Rather than treating tax evasion as a purely economic anomaly or a simple legal violation, the analysis examines how fiscal behavior is shaped by strategic incentives, political institutions, social norms, psychological motivations, and broader processes of institutional legitimacy. This interdisciplinary perspective increasingly characterizes the contemporary literature on tax compliance, which combines economic and psychological approaches in the analysis of fiscal behavior and institutional cooperation. Then, Section 1.7 clarifies the scope of the analysis and the main dimensions left outside the book. Finally, Section 1.8 concludes by reflecting on the multidimensional nature of tax evasion and its implications for fiscal governance and institutional legitimacy.

1.2 The Economic Lens: Incentives, Efficiency, and Distortions

Tax evasion is not an anomaly in economic behavior; rather, it is one of the most studied consequences of taxation itself. From the earliest theoretical contributions, economists have recognized that taxes distort behavior, creating incentives for avoidance, evasion, and changes in labor supply or investment decisions. For example, the Laffer Curve, introduced by Arthur Laffer in the 1970s, famously illustrated the non-linear relationship between tax rates and revenue, suggesting that beyond a certain threshold, higher tax rates may reduce total revenue by encouraging evasion and discouraging productive activity. It is, therefore, not surprising that tax evasion also contributes to the expansion of informal and hidden economic activities, as extensively analyzed in the literature on this topic (Schneider and Enste 2000).

The modern economic literature on tax evasion largely originates from the seminal model developed by Allingham and Sandmo (1972), which conceptualized tax compliance as a rational choice under uncertainty: taxpayers compare the expected benefit of underreporting income with the expected cost, which depends on the probability of detection and the severity of penalties. Although this rationalist framework is formally coherent, it presents a well-known empirical paradox: by relying exclusively on financial deterrence, it tends to predict levels of tax evasion significantly higher than the actual levels of compliance observed in reality. This gap between theoretical predictions and empirical evidence has progressively revealed the limitations of models based solely on monetary incentives and deterrence, paving the way for broader interpretations that assign a central role to institutional trust, social norms, reciprocity, and the perceived quality of public expenditure. The key policy challenge therefore becomes not only how to increase the expected cost of evasion, but also how to build institutional conditions capable of making compliance sustainable and cooperative in the long run.

An optimal punishment framework, therefore, is not sufficient on its own. Detection probabilities and evasion opportunities are heterogeneous; enforcement is costly and politically constrained, while excessive deterrence can erode voluntary cooperation. This implies that punishment parameters must be embedded within a broader institutional architecture where formal coercion and institutional trust function as complementary forces.

The economic analysis of tax evasion extends beyond individual incentives. It addresses welfare distortions, macroeconomic consequences, and the empirical measurement challenges (the latter will be explored in Chapter 3).

From an efficiency perspective, it is useful to distinguish two layers of distortion. On the one hand, taxes create transparent, legislated wedges that can be designed and minimized. On the other hand, evasion creates opaque, uneven wedges that undermine equity, public goods provision, and rule credibility. Even when evasion appears to offset tax burdens in partial equilibrium, its general equilibrium effect is welfare reducing.

These efficiency considerations are closely connected to tax pressure and the way tax systems are designed. The level of taxation and the structure of the tax burden interact with detection risk in shaping the attractiveness of evasion. Simpler tax systems, with moderate and predictable rates, reduce opportunities for arbitrage and make enforcement less costly. Empirical evidence also shows that improvements in administrative efficiency can increase tax revenues even without changes in statutory tax rates, confirming that institutional quality is itself a fundamental policy lever (Pomeranz 2015).

Policy therefore operates along two complementary margins: calibrating effective tax pressure and improving the perceived return on the tax–public goods exchange. Visible, high-quality services increase the payoff to compliance, reducing reliance on coercion. High-pressure regimes with weak service provision, by contrast, amplify evasion incentives and entrench costly deterrence cycles.

Tax policy also performs a signaling function. Rates and enforcement levels communicate state capacity and legitimacy. Lower taxes may signal weakness if not accompanied by credible governance; higher taxes paired with visible public investment may reinforce reciprocity. The effectiveness of fiscal policy thus depends not only on economic incentives but on how policies are interpreted by taxpayers.

1.3 The Political Lens: Legitimacy, Consent, and the Fiscal Contract

Taxation is not merely a financial transaction; it is rather a political act. It expresses the authority of the state and the consent of the governed. From a political perspective, tax evasion challenges the legitimacy of fiscal systems and the credibility of democratic institutions. Seen through the political lens, the strategic noncompliance mirrors a frayed fiscal contract: where legitimacy and reciprocity are weak, individually rational defection becomes collectively rationalized, and rebuilding compliance requires not only sanctions but credible signals of fairness and value.

The fiscal contract theory posits that citizens comply when they perceive taxation as reciprocal (see Section 2.5.2): they pay taxes in exchange for public goods, representation, and institutional fairness. When this contract breaks down, due to corruption, inefficiency, or inequality, evasion becomes a form of protest or disengagement.

A provocative question arises: can tax evasion be a form of political expression? In contexts of low trust, evasion may reflect not greed but grievance. As an example, repeated tax amnesties have arguably eroded the moral authority of the state, signaling that compliance is optional and that evaders will eventually be forgiven (see Section 2.5.3). In such cases, evasion becomes a rational response to a perceived breach of the fiscal contract.

Moreover, evasion has distributive consequences. It shifts the burden onto compliant taxpayers, exacerbates inequality, and erodes trust in the rule of law. In fragile democracies, widespread evasion can undermine state capacity, fuel populist backlash, and destabilize governance (Fergusson et al. 2019).

However, the political economy of tax evasion remains underdeveloped. How does evasion interact with political polarization, populism, and institutional decay? Can compliance be restored without restoring legitimacy? These questions are particularly urgent in an era of democratic backsliding and fiscal austerity. Evasion may not only reflect institutional weakness: it may accelerate it, creating a vicious cycle of mistrust, underfunding, and disengagement.

Understanding tax evasion as a political act invites a broader agenda linking fiscal behavior to democratic health, and compliance to civic belonging. It suggests that restoring compliance requires more than enforcement; it requires rebuilding the moral and institutional foundations of the fiscal state.

1.4 The Sociological Lens: Norms, Identity, and the Social Meaning of Evasion

From a sociological perspective, tax evasion is not merely an individual act of dishonesty; rather, it is a socially embedded behavior shaped by collective norms, institutional relationships, and cultural meanings. Sociology therefore invites us to move beyond a purely economic interpretation of evasion and to examine how social environments influence the legitimacy and acceptability of noncompliance.

At its core, tax evasion also represents a breach of the social (and not only of the fiscal) contract. Modern states rely on tax revenues to finance public goods and collective services, and widespread evasion weakens the relationship of reciprocity between citizens and institutions. When large segments of the population evade taxes, the consequences extend beyond fiscal losses and affect institutional trust and social cohesion more broadly.

Nevertheless, it is important to underline that evasion is not always perceived as a purely criminal or immoral act. In contexts where taxpayers believe that public resources are wasted, corruption is widespread, or economic elites benefit from forms of impunity, tax evasion may be reinterpreted as a reaction to perceived systemic injustice. Under these conditions, the traditional distinction between "honest taxpayers" and "dishonest evaders" tends to become socially more ambiguous and contested (Wenzel 2004; Gòrecki and Letki 2021).

Sociological analysis also highlights the role of social environments in shaping compliance behavior. Individuals do not make fiscal decisions in isolation, but within networks and communities that influence expectations and behavioral standards. Professional groups, local communities, family environments, and informal social networks may all contribute either to reinforcing or weakening compliance norms.

In communities where evasion is widespread and rarely sanctioned, it may gradually become normalized and socially tolerated. Conversely, in contexts where civic duty and contribution to collective welfare are strongly valued, compliance may come to represent a marker of moral reliability and social belonging. These dynamics are further reinforced through informal networks in which information, strategies, and justifications for tax evasion circulate socially (Bobek et al. 2013).

Beyond social interactions, sociology also emphasizes the cultural dimension of taxation. What a society considers "fair" or "unfair" in fiscal behavior is not fixed, but historically and culturally constructed. Collective memories, political traditions, and historical experiences all contribute to shaping how taxation is interpreted and morally evaluated.

In some societies, paying taxes is associated with civic participation and collective solidarity; in others, taxation is viewed with suspicion and perceived as a coercive transfer toward institutions considered inefficient or untrustworthy (Onu and Oats 2016). Cultural attitudes toward the state therefore influence not only individual compliance decisions, but also the broader level of social legitimacy attributed to taxation itself.

The sociological lens therefore suggests that tax evasion cannot be fully understood solely through enforcement and financial incentives. Compliance depends not only on the probability of detection or the severity of penalties, but also on social trust, collective expectations, institutional legitimacy, and culturally embedded perceptions of fairness. Understanding these dimensions is essential for designing tax systems that are not only effective, but also socially sustainable and institutionally credible.

1.5 The Legal Lens: Ambiguity, Enforcement, and Institutional Design

From a legal perspective, tax evasion is not merely a policy challenge, but also a violation of the rule of law. This constitutional dimension is particularly evident in several democratic systems, where the obligation to contribute to public expenditure according to one's economic capacity is explicitly recognized as a foundational principle of fiscal citizenship. The Italian Constitution, for instance, states that all citizens are required to contribute to public expenditure in accordance with their ability to pay (Art.

53). Similar principles can be found in other democratic constitutional systems, such as Spain, where taxation is explicitly linked to economic capacity, equality, and progressivity (Art. 31.1 of the Spanish Constitution).

Legal systems define tax evasion as the intentional concealment of taxable income or fraudulent behavior aimed at reducing tax liability. This includes underreporting, falsifying records, and hiding assets. In this regard, it is useful to recall the distinction between evasion and avoidance. By tax evasion lawyers and policymakers usually refer to the intentional violation of tax law to reduce a legally due liability, which is unlawful and sanctionable. By tax avoidance they usually refer to legally structured practices that exploit gaps across tax systems to erode the base. The distinction matters because it implies different remedies: enforcement for evasion, rule-making and coordination for avoidance. However, although this distinction remains central, it is often blurred in practice: as an example, aggressive tax planning and offshore structures may be formally legal but ethically questionable, raising concerns about fairness and the erosion of the tax base.

Comparative legal analysis also reveals significant variation in how tax evasion is defined, prosecuted, and sanctioned across jurisdictions. In common law systems, such as the United Kingdom and the United States, tax evasion is typically addressed through a combination of administrative penalties and criminal prosecution, with a high burden of proof required for conviction. In contrast, civil law systems, such as those in Italy, France, and Germany, often rely on administrative procedures and presumptive assessments, with criminal liability triggered only above certain thresholds. These differences reflect broader legal cultures and institutional capacities, influencing both enforcement strategies and taxpayer behavior.

The common denominator could (and perhaps should) always be represented by the principle of proportionality, which plays a crucial role in shaping the legitimacy of enforcement. Excessive penalties or intrusive audits may violate constitutional protections, such as due process and privacy rights, especially in democratic societies.

Judicial interpretation also shapes the boundaries of evasion. Courts often play a pivotal role in defining the intent required for criminal liability, the admissibility of evidence, and the scope of administrative discretion. Landmark rulings, such as *Cheek v. United States* (1991) in the U.S.[1] or *Cassazione Penale n. 1235/2018* in Italy[2], have clarified the conditions

[1] Cheek v. United States, 498 U.S. 192 (1991).

[2] Corte di Cassazione Penale, Italy: Verdict n. 1235/2018.

under which ignorance of the law, good faith, or procedural irregularities may mitigate liability. These decisions contribute to the evolving jurisprudence of tax compliance and reflect the tension between deterrence and fairness (D'Agostino et al. 2021).

Nor should it be overlooked that legal design interacts with institutional capacity. Complex and ambiguous tax codes create opportunities for evasion and avoidance, especially when enforcement is uneven or under-resourced. Simplification and codification, such as Italy's efforts to consolidate tax procedures under the "Statuto del contribuente"[3], aim to reduce uncertainty and enhance legal clarity. However, simplification must be balanced with equity: flat taxes or presumptive regimes may reduce complexity but risk undermining progressivity and distributive justice.

In sum, the legal lens reveals that tax evasion is not only a matter of enforcement but also of institutional design, normative legitimacy, and procedural justice. Legal systems must navigate the tension between deterrence and rights protection, between administrative efficiency and constitutional safeguards. Understanding these dynamics is essential for designing tax regimes that are not only effective but also legally and democratically legitimate.

1.6 The Psychological Lens: Morality, Motivation, and the Emotional Cost of Evasion

The psychological dimension of tax evasion has gained increasing prominence in recent years, as scholars have recognized that compliance cannot be fully explained by economic incentives or legal deterrents alone. Instead, tax behavior is deeply intertwined with how individuals perceive fairness, trust institutions, and construct their moral identity. In this view, tax evasion is not only a financial decision, but also a psychological act that carries emotional and moral implications.

A central concept in this literature is tax morale, together with civic duty, solidarity, and the other intrinsic motivations to pay taxes, even in the absence of enforcement. In this context, social norms operate both as external signals that shape expectations about others' behavior and as internalized standards embedded in individual motivation: when taxpayers believe that others are evading, or that the system is corrupt or inefficient, their own motivation to comply tends to erode (see Chapter 2).

[3] L. n. 212/2000, Italy.

Recent research has emphasized the moral cost of evasion, understood as the psychological discomfort associated with dishonest behavior. Andreoni et al. (1998), for example, argue that tax compliance cannot be explained solely through deterrence mechanisms and discuss the role of guilt, shame, social norms, and "psychic costs" in shaping taxpayer behavior. Their review suggests that many individuals comply even when standard deterrence incentives alone would predict higher levels of evasion, highlighting the importance of internalized norms and moral motivations in sustaining compliance.

Conversely, paying taxes can generate positive psychological rewards because, for instance, it can be associated with positive psychological outcomes, framing taxation as a prosocial act that reinforces civic identity and well-being. This raises another provocative question: Does paying taxes make us feel good? Under certain conditions, the answer appears to be yes. When taxes are framed as contributions to a common good, and when institutions are trusted, compliance becomes not only a legal obligation but a moral affirmation. This insight has profound implications for policy design: nudges that emphasize civic identity and perceptions of fairness may be more effective than threats of punishment (Hallsworth et al. 2014; Kirchler 2007).

A growing body of work also explores the heterogeneity of individual motivations. Taxpayers differ in their psychological profiles: some are driven by duty and tax morale, others by deterrence and fear of sanctions, and others still by social comparison and perceptions regarding the behavior of other taxpayers (Molero and Pujol 2012). Understanding these dynamics is therefore important for designing resilient and credible tax systems.

Intrinsic motivations will play a central role in the analysis developed throughout the following chapters. Chapter 2 will explore in detail the psychological foundations of voluntary compliance, examining how intrinsic drivers, such as moral identity, civic pride, and perceived fairness, can be cultivated and sustained over time. These motivations are not static; they evolve in response to political, economic, and institutional shocks. Understanding their dynamics is the key to building resilient tax systems.

In sum, the psychological lens reveals that tax compliance is not just about what people do: it is about how they feel, what they believe, and who they think they are. It invites us to see taxation not only as a fiscal mechanism, but as a moral and emotional practice, embedded in the fabric of democratic life.

1.7 What Remains Outside

Since this work deliberately focuses on the behavioral foundations of tax compliance and the strategic interaction between taxpayers and the state, it does not aim to be exhaustive, nor does it attempt to cover every dimension of tax evasion. Several important areas are intentionally left outside its scope. These exclusions are not omissions, but rather analytical choices, made to preserve coherence, depth, and clarity. Below, I outline the main limitations of the following analysis, explain what each excluded dimension entails, and briefly discuss the existing literature that has addressed them.

1.7.1 International Tax Avoidance and Corporate Profit Shifting

This refers to the strategies used by multinational corporations to minimize their tax liabilities by shifting profits to low-tax jurisdictions, exploiting mismatches in national tax systems, and using complex financial instruments and transfer pricing schemes.

The topic has been extensively studied in the context of the OECD/G20's Base Erosion and Profit Shifting (BEPS) project (2015) and its subsequent global iterations, as well as in works by Zucman (2014), Cobham and Janský (2018), and Alstadsæter et al. (2019). These studies document the scale of global tax avoidance and its impact on revenue losses, inequality, and fiscal sovereignty.

Although some of these themes inevitably intersect with broader discussions developed throughout the book, particularly when addressing tax gap measurement, institutional trust, transparency, and international comparability, they do not constitute its core analytical focus. The primary objective of this volume is instead to examine individual and domestic tax compliance behavior from a behavioral, institutional, and public finance perspective. The mechanisms, actors, and policy tools involved in international corporate tax planning differ substantially from those analyzed here. A systematic treatment of multinational profit shifting and cross-border corporate avoidance would therefore have required a separate analytical framework and would have risked diluting the central behavioral focus of the book.

1.7.2 Historical and Anthropological Perspectives on Tax Evasion

These approaches explore how tax compliance and evasion have evolved over time, how they are embedded in cultural narratives, and how they reflect broader social and political transformations. They often rely on ethnographic methods, archival research, and comparative historical analysis.

Scholars such as Tognato (2015), Schönhärl et al. (2022), and Prichard (2015) have explored how taxation and tax compliance are intertwined with broader processes of state legitimacy, resistance, and adaptation to political authority. These works highlight the symbolic and moral dimensions of taxation, especially in post-authoritarian or post-colonial contexts.

While these perspectives are rich and insightful, they require methodological tools and disciplinary expertise that go beyond the scope of this book. The focus here is on contemporary behavioral dynamics and policy design, not on historical reconstruction or cultural interpretation.

1.7.3 *Administrative and Procedural Tax Law*

This includes the legal rules governing tax audits, appeals, sanctions, taxpayer rights, and procedural safeguards. It also covers the institutional architecture of tax authorities and the legal interpretation of evasion versus avoidance.

The book touches on legal aspects only insofar as they relate to behavioral responses. A full legal analysis would have required a detailed comparative study of tax codes, judicial decisions, and administrative practices—an endeavor incompatible with the behavioral and strategic focus of the volume.

1.7.4 *Macroeconomic and Fiscal Policy Implications*

This approach analyzes the aggregate effects of tax evasion on public finance, debt sustainability, and macroeconomic stability. It includes issues such as the fiscal multiplier, tax buoyancy, and the impact of evasion on redistribution and inequality. In the macroeconomic literature, however, the emphasis is often placed more broadly on the concept of the shadow or underground economy, of which tax evasion represents only one component. In this context, scholars such as Tanzi (1999) and Schneider and Enste (2000) have examined the macroeconomic implications of hidden economic activity, highlighting their effects on public revenues, fiscal sustainability, redistribution, and public sector performance.

While the book acknowledges the systemic impact of evasion, it does not develop a macroeconomic model. The emphasis is on micro-level behavior and institutional interaction, not on aggregate fiscal dynamics.

Nevertheless, the measurement of tax evasion, which partly intersects with the macroeconomic dimension of the phenomenon, will be examined in Chapter 3, particularly with reference to the methodological challenges involved in estimating hidden fiscal behavior.

1.7.5 Taxation in the Digital Economy

This includes the challenges posed by digital platforms, cryptocurrencies, and cross-border e-commerce to traditional tax enforcement. It also involves the use of AI, big data, and real-time reporting in tax administration.

The OECD (2021) and van Liebergen (2017) have explored how digitalization transforms both evasion opportunities and enforcement capabilities.

The book discusses digital tools only in relation to behavioral nudges and transparency dashboards. A full treatment of digital taxation would require a separate technical and regulatory analysis, which falls outside the scope of this volume.

1.8 Concluding Reflections

As shown above, tax evasion is a multidimensional phenomenon shaped by economic incentives, political legitimacy, social norms, legal ambiguity, and psychological perceptions. No single disciplinary lens is sufficient to capture its complexity in full.

This chapter has argued that understanding tax compliance requires moving beyond purely technical or deterrence-based explanations. Compliance emerges from the interaction between institutional structures, individual motivations, and broader social expectations. The chapters that follow build on this perspective by examining how enforcement and intrinsic motivations interact, how evasion is measured, and how different institutional environments may influence compliance behavior over time.

More broadly, the analysis suggests that sustainable tax compliance depends not only on effective enforcement, but also on the capacity of public institutions to maintain credibility, transparency, and cooperative expectations between citizens and the state.

References

Alstadsæter, A., Johannesen, N. & Zucman, G. (2019). Tax Evasion and Inequality. *American Economic Review* 109(6), 2073–2103.

Allingham, M. G. & Sandmo, A. (1972). Income Tax Evasion: A Theoretical Analysis. *Journal of Public Economics* 1(3–4), 323–338.

Andreoni, J., Erard, B. & Feinstein, J. (1998). Tax Compliance. *Journal of Economic Literature* 36(2), 818–860.

Besley, T. & Persson, T. (2014). Why do Developing Countries Tax so Little? *Journal of Economic Perspectives* 28(4), 99–120.

Bobek, D. D., Hageman, A. M. & Kelliher, C. F. (2013). Analyzing the Role of Social Norms in Tax Compliance Behavior. *Journal of Business Ethics* 115(3), 451–468.

Cobham, A & Janský, P. (2018). Global Distribution of Revenue Loss from Corporate Tax Avoidance: Re-estimation and Country Results. *Journal of International Development 30*(2), 206–232.

D'Agostino, E., De Benedetto, M. A. & Sobbrio, G. (2021). Tax Evasion and Government Size: Evidence from Italian Provinces. *Economia Politica* 38(3), 1149–1187.

Feld, L. P. & Frey, B. S. (2007). Tax Compliance as the Result of a Psychological Tax Contract: The Role of Incentives and Responsive Regulation. *Law & Policy* 29(1), 102–120.

Fergusson, L., Molina, C. & Riaño, J. F. (2019). Consumers as VAT Evaders: Incidence, Social Bias, and Correlates in Colombia. *Economia* 19(2), 21–68.

Gòrecki, M. A & Letki N. (2021). Social Norms Moderate the Effect of Tax System on Tax Evasion: Evidence from a Large-Scale Survey Experiment. *Journal of Business Ethics* 172, 727–746.

Hallsworth, M., List, J. A., Metcalfe, R. D. & Vlaev, I. (2014). The Behavioralist as Tax Collector: Using Natural Field Experiments to Enhance Tax Compliance. *Journal of Public Economics* 117, 14–31.

Kirchler, E. (2007). *The Economic Psychology of Tax Behaviour.* Cambridge University Press.

Levi, M. (1988). *Of Rule and Revenue.* University of California Press.

Molero, J. C. & Pujol, F. (2012). Walking Inside the Potential Tax Evader's Mind: Tax Morale does Matter. *Journal of Business Ethics* 105(2), 151–162.

OECD/G20 (2015), *Explanatory Statement: OECD/G20 Base Erosion and Profit Shifting Project*, OECD Publishing, Paris.

OECD (2021). *Two-Pillar Solution to Address the Tax Challenges Arising from the Digitalisation of the Economy.* OECD Publishing, Paris.

Onu, D. & Oats, L. (2016). Paying Tax is Part of Life: Social Norms and Social Influence in Tax Communications. *Journal of Economic Behavior and Organization* 124, 29–42.

Pomeranz, D. (2015). "No Taxation without Information: Deterrence and Self-Enforcement in the Value Added Tax." *American Economic Review* 105(8), 2539–2569.

Prichard, W. (2015). *Taxation, Responsiveness and Accountability in Sub-Saharan Africa: The Dynamics of Tax Bargaining*. Cambridge University Press.

Schneider, F., & Enste, D. H. (2000). Shadow Economies: Size, Causes, and Consequences. *Journal of Economic Literature* 38(1), 77–114.

Schönhärl, K., Hurlimann, G. & Rohde, D. (2022). *Histories of Tax Evasion, Avoidance, and Resistance*. Routledge.

Tanzi, V. (1999). Uses and Abuses of Estimates of the Underground Economy. *The Economic Journal* 109(456), 338–347.

Tognato, C. (2015). Narratives of Tax Evasion: The Cultural legitimacy of Harmful Behavior. In L. Presser and S. Sandberg (Eds.), Narrative Criminology: Understanding Stories of Crime (pp. 260–286). New York University Press.

Van Liebergen, B. (2017). Machine Learning: A Revolution in Risk-Management and Compliance? *Journal of Financial Transformation* 45, 60–67.

Wenzel, M (2004). An Analysis of Norm Processes in Tax Compliance. *Journal of Economic Psychology* 25(2), 213–228.

Zucman, G. (2014). Taxing Across Borders: Tracking Personal Wealth and Corporate Profits. *Journal of Economic Perspectives 28*(4), 121–148.

CHAPTER 2

External Incentives and Intrinsic Motivations

Abstract This chapter examines the behavioral and institutional foundations of tax compliance, moving beyond traditional deterrence-based approaches centered exclusively on audits and penalties. The analysis focuses on key concepts such as tax morale, reciprocity, institutional trust, civic duty, and social norms, emphasizing how these factors interact in shaping voluntary compliance.

Particular attention is devoted to the relationship between taxpayers and public institutions, exploring how perceptions of fairness, legitimacy, and public goods provision influence compliance behavior. The chapter also discusses the role of motivational postures, crowding-out effects, and the interaction between enforcement and trust, showing how excessive coercion may undermine intrinsic motivations under certain institutional conditions.

The chapter highlights the heterogeneity of taxpayer responses and the importance of contextual factors in shaping compliance dynamics. International evidence and policy experiences are integrated throughout the discussion to illustrate how different institutional environments may generate markedly different patterns of cooperation, resistance, and fiscal legitimacy.

Keywords Deterrence theory • Tax morale • Trust in institutions • Slippery Slope Framework • Motivational postures

E. D'Agostino, *The Determinants of Tax Evasion*, Palgrave Studies in Institutions, Economics and Law,
https://doi.org/10.1007/978-3-032-21897-1_2

2.1 Introduction

Tax compliance emerges from the interaction between deterrence mechanisms, institutional conditions, and individual motivations. While classical economic approaches emphasize enforcement, audit probability, and penalties, behavioral and institutional perspectives highlight the role of trust, civic duty, social norms, and perceptions of fairness. Understanding how these dimensions interact is essential for designing tax policies capable of sustaining voluntary compliance alongside formal enforcement.

This chapter examines the main determinants of tax compliance through economic, behavioral, psychological, and sociological perspectives. Particular attention is devoted to the interaction between deterrence mechanisms and behavioral dimensions of compliance, including recent evidence on nudges and field interventions (see Antinyan and Asatryan 2025 for a comprehensive meta-analysis).

The Allingham and Sandmo's (1972) approach laid the foundation for deterrence theory, which remains a cornerstone of tax policy. Enforcement mechanisms, such as audits and fines, are designed to increase the expected cost of noncompliance, thereby increasing incentives to comply. Empirical research (Slemrod et al. 2001; Alm et al. 1992) demonstrates that compliance generally rises with higher audit probabilities and stricter penalties, supporting the basic predictions of classical deterrence models.

However, evidence increasingly shows that enforcement alone cannot fully explain observed levels of compliance (Tyler 1990), highlighting the importance of accounting for taxpayer heterogeneity and the potentially unequal effects of behavioral interventions across different socioeconomic groups (Deparade et al. 2025). In this regard, many taxpayers comply even when the probability of detection is low, while some evade despite high audit risk. This discrepancy suggests that taxpayer behavior cannot be explained exclusively through deterrence.

Among the most important non-deterrence factors are tax morale, institutional trust, and civic duty, which influence compliance beyond formal enforcement mechanisms.

The interaction between deterrence and intrinsic motivations also has important policy implications. Excessively punitive enforcement may weaken institutional trust and reduce cooperative attitudes, whereas transparent and credible institutions can strengthen voluntary compliance and complement traditional deterrence mechanisms. Digitalization and behavioral nudges increasingly operate within this broader strategic perspective (see Section 2.4.6).

In sum, tax compliance cannot be understood exclusively through deterrence-based models. Economic incentives, institutional credibility, social norms, and individual motivations interact in shaping heterogeneous compliance behaviors across different contexts. The following sections examine these dimensions progressively, distinguishing between external incentives, intrinsic motivations, behavioral frameworks, and institutional signals, while emphasizing their interdependence rather than treating them as isolated determinants of compliance.

2.2 External Incentives

Repression is arguably the oldest and, in some respects, the most straightforward expression of state power. Since the earliest civilizations, rulers have relied on coercive mechanisms to extract resources from their subjects.

In ancient Egypt, for instance, tax collectors were so feared that they were often depicted in tomb paintings wielding sticks: an early and literal representation of the "stick" in the carrot-and-stick approach. In Mesopotamia, tax evasion could lead to severe punishments, including forced labor or confiscation of property. Even in ancient Rome, tax collectors (*publicani*) were notorious for their aggressive methods, to the extent that the term "publican" became synonymous with corruption and extortion. While such practices may seem draconian or even darkly humorous from a modern democratic perspective, they underscore the historical continuity of enforcement as a central tool of fiscal governance.

Turning to modern tax systems, external incentives have traditionally constituted the foundation for understanding tax compliance within the economic literature. These incentives are grounded in classical economic theory, which posits that individuals act rationally, evaluating the potential gains from evading taxes against the expected costs associated with detection and penalties. Tax evasion thus becomes one of the possible outcomes of a probabilistic gamble, occurring when the expected costs of compliance are lower than the expected benefits of evasion (Allingham and Sandmo 1972).

According to this classical perspective, audit probability is therefore a critical determinant of compliance. If taxpayers perceive a high likelihood of inspection, the expected cost of evasion increases, thereby enhancing compliance. Similarly, the severity of penalties, including fines, interest, and legal sanctions, directly influences taxpayer behavior.

Empirical studies provide mixed evidence on these predictions: Friedland et al. (1978), using a simulation experiment, found that while higher audit probabilities do reduce evasion, the deterrent effect of severe penalties is even stronger, suggesting that enforcement design should consider both dimensions rather than focusing solely on audit frequency. More broadly, Slemrod (2007) emphasized the central role of enforcement mechanisms in shaping tax compliance behavior and discussed the limits of purely deterrence-based approaches.

However, the literature also suggests that enforcement effects may be non-linear: beyond a certain threshold, increasing audit intensity can produce diminishing marginal returns, highlighting the importance of optimizing enforcement strategies relative to resource constraints (Slemrod and Yitzhaki 2002).

Contemporary research has extended classical models by incorporating heterogeneity in risk preferences and taxpayer characteristics. Individuals differ in risk aversion, their perception of detection probabilities, and access to evasion opportunities. High-income taxpayers and multinational corporations, for example, often have greater capacity to evade through sophisticated financial structures, including profit shifting and offshore accounts (Hanlon and Heitzman 2010). Small firms and informal sector participants, in contrast, may have fewer resources but higher exposure to audits, creating differential compliance incentives. These findings underscore the necessity of tailoring enforcement policies to specific taxpayer segments to achieve efficiency and equity.

Modern approaches also emphasize dynamic considerations and repeated interactions between taxpayers and tax authorities. Compliance behavior is influenced not only by immediate enforcement but also by learning from past experiences and by expectations regarding future audit probabilities and enforcement credibility. Multi-period and game-theoretic models show that taxpayers adjust their behavior over time in response to observed audit outcomes and perceived enforcement strategies, highlighting the importance of designing long-term and strategically coherent compliance policies (Andreoni et al. 1998).

A crucial distinction in the literature on external incentives concerns the difference between coercive and reputational/informational mechanisms. On the one hand, coercive incentives rely on the threat or application of sanctions (like audits, fines, and legal prosecution) to deter noncompliance. These are the traditional instruments of deterrence, grounded in the logic of expected utility maximization. On the other hand, reputational and informational incentives operate through perception, signaling, and social influence. They do not impose direct costs but shape taxpayer behavior by altering beliefs about enforcement, fairness, and social norms. For example, media coverage of high-profile tax evasion cases can increase perceived detection risk and reinforce compliance norms. Similarly, public campaigns that highlight peer compliance or the civic value of taxation can activate reputational concerns and conditional cooperation (Hallsworth et al. 2014).

Tax authorities increasingly use strategic communication tools, such as personalized reminders, transparency dashboards, and behavioral nudges, to influence taxpayer psychology. These interventions are often low-cost and scalable, and they can complement coercive enforcement by enhancing its perceived legitimacy. In contexts where institutional trust is fragile or enforcement capacity is limited, reputational and informational incentives may be particularly effective in sustaining compliance.

In sum, external incentives encompass both coercive mechanisms, which deter evasion through the threat of punishment, and informational/reputational mechanisms, which influence behavior through perception and social signaling. Effective tax policy requires a calibrated mix of both, recognizing that taxpayer decisions are shaped not only by actual enforcement but also by how enforcement is communicated, interpreted, and socially embedded.

2.3 Intrinsic Motivations

2.3.1 Introduction

Interpreting tax compliance solely as the effect of deterrence mechanisms such as audits and penalties is now widely considered reductive. In many contexts, individuals comply with tax obligations even when enforcement is weak or the probability of audit is low. This observation has led to a growing recognition of the role of intrinsic motivations as internalized psychological, ethical, and social drivers that influence compliance independently of external coercion (Torgler 2007).

Among these, tax morale is perhaps the most studied. It refers to the intrinsic willingness to pay taxes, shaped by ethical convictions, perceptions of fairness, and a sense of social responsibility (Bordignon 1993; Luttmer and Singhal 2014). High tax morale helps explain, for example, why some taxpayers remain compliant even in the absence of strong enforcement.

Tax morale is not static; it evolves in response to a combination of institutional signals and socioeconomic conditions. Fair, consistent, and transparent enforcement can reinforce tax morale by signaling institutional legitimacy, while arbitrary or excessively punitive measures may weaken it by undermining perceived fairness and reciprocity (Frey and Jegen 2001; Kirchler et al. 2008; see Section 2.4). At the same time, broader socioeconomic and cultural factors, such as education, civic socialization, and exposure to ethical norms, tend to strengthen intrinsic motivation, whereas systemic inequities, favoritism, and perceived mismanagement can erode it.

Closely related to tax morale is trust in institutions, defined as the belief that tax authorities and public institutions act competently, fairly, and in the public interest. Trust operates at both individual and collective levels, shaping perceptions of institutional credibility, influencing expectations about others' behavior, and reducing reliance on coercive enforcement (Kirchler et al. 2008; Luttmer and Singhal 2014). Trust in institutions is also shaped through repeated interactions with public authorities and by perceptions of transparency, communication, and responsiveness.

Another key intrinsic motivation is civic duty, which reflects a normative commitment to contribute to the public good. While tax morale is often grounded in fairness and reciprocity, civic duty emphasizes moral obligation and social responsibility. It emerges through long-term processes of education, cultural transmission, and socialization, which shape individuals' perceptions of what constitutes responsible behavior within a society. Civic duty therefore embodies a normative orientation toward cooperation, respect for common rules, and concern for the functioning of social institutions: individuals with a strong sense of civic duty pay taxes not because they fear punishment, but because they view it as a fundamental aspect of citizenship (Braithwaite 2003).

Social norms and conditional cooperation are further important drivers of human behavior in general and of the tax compliance decision in particular. Taxpayers often calibrate their behavior based on what they perceive others are doing. When compliance is the norm, individuals are more likely to follow suit, especially if institutions are seen as fair and competent (Frey and Torgler 2007; Kirchler 2007). These feedback loops can generate relatively stable patterns of compliance. However, in heterogeneous societies where evasion is visible and tolerated in some groups, social norms may conflict with civic duty, undermining intrinsic motivation.

To address these tensions, policymakers can implement interventions that strengthen positive norms and reduce perceived inequities. Measures such as community-level reporting on compliance rates, participatory mechanisms, and increased transparency in public spending can support intrinsic motivation and align individual behavior with collective outcomes.

2.3.2 *Interaction of Intrinsic Motivations*

Intrinsic motivations do not operate in isolation but interact in ways that may reinforce or weaken tax compliance outcomes. In particular, tax morale is closely related to institutional trust and perceptions of legitimacy. High levels of trust in public institutions tend to strengthen voluntary compliance, whereas low trust may foster skepticism, resistance, or evasion, even in the presence of formal enforcement mechanisms (Alm and Torgler 2006; Feld and Frey 2007).

Civic duty also interacts with other intrinsic motivations in ways that depend on the broader institutional and social environment. First, civic duty interacts with tax morale: when individuals perceive taxation as both fair and socially necessary, their intrinsic motivation to comply is reinforced. Second, it can help sustain compliance even in contexts where institutional trust is low, acting as a moral anchor that compensates for perceived inefficiencies or corruption. Its effectiveness is strengthened when aligned with favorable social norms, but it may weaken when individuals perceive that others are not contributing fairly.

Social norms interact with other intrinsic motivations as well by shaping how individuals interpret the behavior of others and adjust their own compliance decisions. When perceptions of widespread compliance align with trust and civic duty, cooperative behavior is reinforced (Frey and Torgler 2007). However, heterogeneity in observed behavior, such as visible evasion among certain groups, can generate conflicting signals, weakening the effectiveness of both social norms and other intrinsic motivations (Fortin et al. 2007; Fellner et al. 2013).

These interactions highlight that intrinsic motivations operate as a dynamic and context-sensitive system, where the strength of each component depends on its alignment with others. Effective policy must therefore account for how these motivations reinforce or counteract one another. For example, promoting transparency and ethical governance can simultaneously enhance trust and tax morale, while public campaigns emphasizing positive peer behavior can strengthen civic duty and social norms. Conversely, perceptions of corruption or inefficiency can weaken trust, undermining both civic duty and tax morale.

In sum, intrinsic motivations form an interdependent motivational architecture, where interactions between trust, civic duty, and social norms generate complex behavioral patterns. These dynamics are essential for designing compliance strategies that reflect both the heterogeneity of taxpayers and the multifaceted nature of intrinsic motivation.

2.3.3 *Theoretical Integration and Feedback Loops*

Beyond their direct interaction, intrinsic motivations may also generate dynamic feedback mechanisms capable of stabilizing or destabilizing tax compliance over time. Tax morale, institutional trust, civic duty, and social norms do not simply coexist: they continuously influence one another through cumulative processes that may reinforce cooperative behavior or, conversely, progressively erode voluntary compliance.

In high-compliance institutional environments, positive feedback loops may emerge. High levels of institutional trust and perceived fairness strengthen tax morale and civic duty, encouraging voluntary compliance. When compliant behavior becomes widespread and socially visible, social norms increasingly reinforce cooperation, further consolidating trust and intrinsic motivation. Over time, these mutually reinforcing dynamics may generate relatively stable patterns of high compliance and institutional legitimacy. As discussed more concretely in the following section, Scandinavian countries are often presented in the literature as approximate examples of this type of virtuous cycle, where transparent governance, effective public service provision, and strong civic norms contribute to sustaining high levels of voluntary compliance (Torgler 2007; OECD 2021).

In these contexts, enforcement itself tends to be perceived as legitimate and proportionate rather than purely coercive. As a result, deterrence complements rather than substitutes for intrinsic motivations, strengthening the credibility of institutions and reinforcing cooperative expectations between taxpayers and the state.

Conversely, negative feedback loops may gradually destabilize compliance. When taxpayers perceive corruption, inefficiency, unfair treatment, or weak reciprocity in the fiscal exchange, institutional trust tends to decline. This erosion weakens tax morale and civic duty, reducing voluntary compliance and increasing tolerance toward opportunistic behavior. As evasion becomes more widespread or socially visible, social norms may progressively normalize noncompliance, further weakening intrinsic motivations and cooperative expectations.

These dynamics may generate path-dependent processes in which deteriorating trust and declining compliance reinforce one another over time. Once such negative loops become entrenched, rebuilding cooperative fiscal relationships may require prolonged institutional reforms and sustained investments in transparency, fairness, administrative credibility, and civic engagement. Similar mechanisms are often discussed in relation to institutional environments characterized by persistent corruption, fragmented administrative capacity, and weak reciprocal expectations between citizens and public institutions.

Understanding these feedback mechanisms is important because they suggest that tax compliance policies should not be evaluated solely according to their immediate deterrence effects. Policies may also influence the long-term evolution of trust, reciprocity, social norms, and institutional legitimacy, thereby shaping the future sustainability of voluntary compliance itself. The policy implications of these dynamics will be examined more explicitly in Section 2.3.5.

More broadly, the existence of both positive and negative feedback loops highlights the fundamentally dynamic nature of tax compliance. Compliance is not simply the outcome of isolated individual decisions, but rather the product of evolving interactions between psychological motivations, social expectations, and institutional environments.

2.3.4 International Evidence on the Coexistence of Intrinsic Motivations

Cross-country studies have shown that tax morale varies significantly and is positively correlated with institutional quality, trust in government, and the perceived effectiveness of public services. This suggests, in turn, that voluntary tax compliance is more sustainable when **intrinsic motivations** and institutional incentives are aligned and mutually reinforcing (Torgler 2007).

For instance, Scandinavian countries consistently exhibit high levels of tax morale, supported by transparent governance, low corruption, and robust welfare systems.

Furthermore, the case of Germany illustrates how strong institutional credibility, stable reciprocal expectations, and widespread adherence to civic norms can support relatively high levels of tax compliance over time. In such contexts, compliance is not driven exclusively by deterrence, but also by the perception that taxation forms part of a broader and functioning social contract. The combination of credible enforcement, administrative efficiency, and internalized cooperative norms contributes to relatively stable compliance patterns and reduces incentives toward opportunistic behavior.

Japan, by contrast, highlights the importance of social cohesion and collective responsibility in sustaining tax compliance. In this context, compliance is reinforced not only by formal institutions, but also by strong reputational concerns, social expectations, and deeply embedded norms of civic contribution. These informal mechanisms complement enforcement policies contributing to relatively stable compliance patterns.

By contrast, the case of Italy reflects a more fragile compliance equilibrium, characterized by heterogeneous patterns of adherence and weaker reciprocal expectations between taxpayers and public institutions. In this context, perceived inefficiencies, institutional fragmentation, and expectations of opportunistic behavior may undermine cooperative compliance dynamics. As a result, enforcement policies often coexist with lower levels of fiscal reciprocity and less stable compliance norms.

These examples underscore that the coexistence of intrinsic motivations is not automatic, but depends on the alignment between institutional conditions and social norms. Where these elements reinforce each other, compliance can become self-sustaining; where they are fragmented, the state may need to rely more heavily on enforcement or risk systemic noncompliance.

2.3.5 Policy Implications and Strategic Integration

The analysis conducted so far suggests that governments aiming to enhance voluntary compliance should adopt integrated strategies that simultaneously strengthen multiple intrinsic motivations.

Transparency initiatives that make the use of public resources more visible can reinforce trust, civic duty, and tax morale by strengthening the perceived link between taxation and public goods (OECD 2021; Kirchler 2007). Participatory mechanisms may further enhance these effects by fostering greater engagement between citizens and public institutions (Allegretti et al. 2021; Manes-Rossi et al. 2023). For example, governments that publish detailed accounts of tax revenue allocation or involve citizens in budgetary decisions demonstrate competence and fairness, thereby reinforcing trust and strengthening intrinsic compliance motivation. Digital platforms offer new opportunities for trust-building by enabling real-time monitoring of public spending and participatory governance.

In addition, educational campaigns emphasizing the ethical foundations of taxation and its social benefits can cultivate a stronger sense of civic responsibility, particularly among younger generations. Social norms can be leveraged through behavioral interventions, such as providing normative information about compliance rates or recognizing compliant taxpayers publicly, which activate conditional cooperation mechanisms (Hallsworth et al. 2014).

Finally, enforcement should remain proportionate and predictable. Excessive or arbitrary measures risk undermining intrinsic motivations, whereas moderate and consistent enforcement can complement and reinforce them (Frey and Jegen 2001; Kirchler et al. 2008).

2.4 Behavioral Frameworks

2.4.1 Introduction to Behavioral Approaches

The previous section explored the role of intrinsic motivations in shaping voluntary tax compliance. While these factors provide a foundational understanding of why individuals may choose to comply even in the absence of strong enforcement, they do not fully capture the dynamic and context-sensitive nature of taxpayer behavior.

This section builds on those insights by introducing behavioral frameworks, intended as structured models that integrate psychological, sociological, and institutional variables to explain how individuals perceive, interpret, and respond to tax obligations. Unlike the more static conceptualization of intrinsic motivations, behavioral frameworks emphasize how motivations interact with enforcement, communication, and institutional design over time, often producing non-linear and heterogeneous outcomes.

Behavioral approaches offer a more operational and potentially predictive lens, enabling policymakers to segment taxpayers, anticipate behavioral responses, and design interventions that align with both intrinsic and extrinsic drivers. They also provide tools to understand how compliance behavior evolves, how trust and legitimacy are built or eroded, and how enforcement strategies can either reinforce or undermine voluntary compliance.

In the following sections, I explore influential behavioral frameworks and psychological principles that have significantly shaped the study of tax compliance:

- *Motivational Postures* (Braithwaite 2003), which categorize taxpayers based on their multi-dimensional psychological stance and social distance toward tax authorities;
- The *Slippery Slope Framework* (Kirchler et al. 2008), which models compliance as a dynamic function of the dialectic interaction between the authorities' power (both coercive and legitimate) and institutional trust;
- The psychological principle of *crowding-out effects* (Frey and Jegen 2001), which provides the micro-foundations for these models by highlighting how coercive enforcement can inadvertently diminish or extinguish intrinsic tax morale.

Together, these theoretical contributions provide a multidimensional understanding of taxpayer behavior and offer practical insights for designing more effective, context-sensitive, and legitimacy-enhancing tax policies.

2.4.2 Motivational Postures

Among behavioral frameworks, motivational postures, developed by Braithwaite (2003), offer a practical tool for segmenting taxpayers according to their attitudes toward authority and compliance obligations. Motivational Postures are defined as psychologically distinct stances that individuals adopt toward tax authorities, reflecting their perception of legitimacy, fairness, and relational dynamics. Unlike static measures of compliance, postures are dynamic and context-dependent, providing insights into how taxpayers might respond to enforcement, communication, and participatory interventions.

Braithwaite identifies five key postures:

1. Commitment: taxpayers comply willingly and perceive taxation as a legitimate social obligation.
2. Capitulation: compliance is motivated by recognition of the legitimacy and authority of tax institutions, leading taxpayers to comply out of acceptance of institutional power and social order.

3. Resistance: taxpayers comply reluctantly and are skeptical of authorities, sometimes showing a tendency to challenge or resist compliance expectations.
4. Disengagement: taxpayers withdraw from institutional engagement, often reflecting distrust and marginalization.
5. Game-playing: taxpayers actively explore loopholes or exploit legal ambiguities to minimize their tax burden. They view compliance not through an ethical lens, approaching taxation as a strategic and technical exercise centered on exploiting legal complexity and minimizing liabilities.

These postures provide a pragmatic lens for both analysis and policy design. For example, taxpayers exhibiting Commitment and Capitulation are more likely to respond positively to transparency and participatory initiatives, reinforcing intrinsic motivations. In contrast, those displaying Resistance require targeted procedural justice and tailored communication to rebuild depleted institutional trust. Meanwhile, taxpayers characterized by Game-playing attitudes require more robust enforcement and clearer regulation to limit opportunities for strategic tax minimization.

Critically, some applications of the Motivational Postures framework may risk treating these orientations as mutually exclusive categories, potentially oversimplifying the complexity and fluidity of taxpayer behavior. In practice, as emphasized in Braithwaite's foundational research, postures can coexist within individuals or populations, and may shift over time in response to perceived fairness, enforcement actions, or social norms. For example, a taxpayer initially resistant may develop higher Commitment following participatory budget experiences, illustrating the dynamic interplay between intrinsic motivation and behavioral framing.

2.4.3 The Slippery Slope Framework

The Slippery Slope Framework (SSF) developed by Kirchler et al. (2008) offers a behavioral model that integrates two fundamental dimensions of tax compliance: power and trust. Unlike classical deterrence models that focus solely on enforcement, the SSF emphasizes that compliance is not only a function of the perceived probability of detection and severity of penalties, but also of the perceived legitimacy, fairness, and competence of tax authorities.

The framework conceptualizes compliance as the outcome of a dynamic interaction between:

- Power of authorities: the capacity to detect and punish noncompliance through audits, fines, and legal sanctions;
- Trust in authorities: the belief that tax institutions act fairly, transparently, and in the public interest.

The dynamic interaction between these two dimensions shifts the fiscal ecosystem along a continuum, shaping different compliance regimes associated with prevailing tax climates:

- *Enforced Compliance*: Driven primarily by the authorities' power, where taxpayers cooperate out of deterrence, monitoring, and fear of penalties. This regime typically capitalizes on an *Antagonistic Tax Climate* (often associated with High Power, Low Trust), where the relationship between citizens and the state is transactional and coercive.
- *Voluntary Compliance:* Sustained by institutional trust, where taxpayers cooperate spontaneously out of civic duty, psychological identification, and perceived legitimacy. This regime thrives within a Synergistic Tax Climate (High (legitimate) Power, High Trust), where effective enforcement protects honest citizens from free-riding; alternatively, it may sustain cooperation in low-power environments where high institutional trust substitutes for limited monitoring capacity, although such equilibria remain institutionally fragile.

When both power and trust are depleted, the fiscal social contract may deteriorate severely, leaving the system trapped in a sort of low-cooperation equilibrium characterized by pervasive evasion and uncoordinated noncompliance.

The SSF provides several key insights for policy design:

- Enforcement is necessary but not sufficient. In high-trust environments, moderate enforcement can be highly effective. In contrast, in low-trust contexts, even intensive enforcement may fail to produce sustainable compliance.

- Trust is dynamic and policy-sensitive. It can be cultivated through transparency, procedural fairness, and consistent institutional behavior.
- An excessive reliance on deterrence may unintentionally undermine cooperative attitudes and weaken the institutional foundations of voluntary compliance.

Empirical evidence supports the SSF's predictions. Cross-country studies show that trust amplifies the effectiveness of enforcement: countries with high institutional trust tend to achieve higher compliance with lower enforcement intensity (Richardson 2006; Torgler 2007). Experimental research further confirms that when taxpayers perceive tax authorities as fair and competent, they are more likely to comply even in the absence of strong deterrents (Wahl et al. 2010).

The SSF also introduces a temporal and relational dimension to compliance. Trust evolves through repeated interactions with institutions and is shaped by the perceived fairness of enforcement, the quality of public services, and the behavior of peers. For example, if enforcement is perceived as arbitrary or excessive, trust may erode, shifting taxpayers from a high trust–high power climate to a high power–low trust one, with negative consequences for long-term compliance.

Finally, the SSF complements other behavioral models. While Motivational Postures focus on individual psychological orientations toward authority, the SSF situates these orientations within broader institutional and enforcement contexts, offering a bridge between micro-level behavior and macro-level policy. For instance, a taxpayer with a resistant posture may still comply when embedded in an institutional environment characterized by high trust and legitimate authority.

2.4.4 Crowding-Out Effects and Enforcement Interactions

A central insight from behavioral economics is that more enforcement does not always mean more compliance. This counterintuitive idea is captured by the concept of crowding-out effects, which occur when coercive enforcement undermines intrinsic motivations such as tax morale, civic duty, or trust in institutions (Frey 1997; Frey and Jegen 2001). While traditional models assume that increasing audits and penalties linearly boosts compliance, behavioral research suggests that excessive or poorly designed enforcement can backfire, especially among taxpayers who are already inclined to comply voluntarily.

Most treatments of crowding-out focus on the psychological mechanism: enforcement signals mistrust, reframing tax compliance from a civic duty into a transactional or adversarial exchange. However, this explanation, while valid, may obscure deeper institutional and communicative dynamics. For instance, the framing of enforcement, that is whether it is perceived as fair, respectful, and proportionate, can significantly moderate its impact. Enforcement that is procedurally fair may generate "crowding-in effects"; in fact, it may reinforce intrinsic motivations by affirming the legitimacy of the system.

Moreover, the timing and sequencing of enforcement matter. Introducing harsh penalties in a context where trust has not yet been established may trigger defensive reactions and resistance. Conversely, if enforcement follows a period of trust-building, for example through transparency, participatory governance, or improved service delivery, it may be interpreted as a necessary safeguard rather than a hostile act.

Rather than abandoning enforcement, behavioral insights call for its recalibration. Enforcement should be:

- Transparent: clearly communicated, with understandable rules and procedures.
- Proportionate: avoiding excessive penalties that may appear punitive rather than corrective.
- Responsive: sensitive to differences in motivational postures and institutional trust, allowing communication and enforcement strategies to be adapted to heterogeneous taxpayer contexts.
- Complemented: by trust-building measures such as participatory budgeting, feedback on public spending, and ethical leadership.

Digital tools offer new opportunities to reshape the experience of compliance, not only by supporting enforcement but also by reducing frictions in taxpayer interactions with the system. For example, pre-filled tax returns, real-time feedback on compliance status, and personalized nudges can make the compliance process feel more like guided participation than punitive monitoring. Importantly, many of these instruments, especially pre-filled returns, primarily function as tools of administrative simplification, lowering compliance costs rather than directly enhancing enforcement per se.

However, their integration must be carefully managed. When digital assistance is transparently communicated and perceived as supportive rather than intrusive, it can preserve the dignity of the taxpayer and reinforce cooperative norms. This relational dimension, often underemphasized in traditional enforcement models, is central to sustaining intrinsic motivation and fostering long-term voluntary compliance.

Despite its conceptual appeal, the crowding-out hypothesis remains relatively difficult to assess empirically, particularly in longitudinal and cross-national settings. Much of the existing evidence relies on short-term experimental designs or self-reported attitudes, which may limit our ability to evaluate its long-term fiscal implications in real-world contexts.

Future research should therefore aim to:

- Quantify the long-term fiscal impact of crowding-out dynamics;
- Explore potential threshold effects, identifying the conditions under which enforcement begins to erode intrinsic motivation;
- Investigate interaction effects between enforcement, trust, and social norms across different taxpayer segments and institutional environments.

In sum, the crowding-out perspective challenges the simplified assumption that more enforcement necessarily leads to higher compliance. Instead, it invites policymakers to adopt a relational rather than purely mechanical approach, recognizing that the legitimacy of enforcement is as important as its intensity. Accordingly, effective tax administration requires carefully calibrated strategies that support, rather than inadvertently erode, intrinsic motivations and perceptions of fairness over time.

2.4.5 Integrating Behavioral Frameworks and Policy Implications

The behavioral frameworks explored so far, and precisely Motivational Postures, the Slippery Slope Framework, and crowding-out effects, are often treated as separate lenses. Yet, their true potential emerges when they are integrated into an integrated behavioral architecture. This integration allows for a more sophisticated understanding of taxpayer behavior, one that moves beyond linear cause-effect models and embraces the complexity, heterogeneity, and adaptability of human decision-making.

Not all taxpayers react to coercive signals in the same way. Using Braithwaite's (2003) terminology, high-morale taxpayers may be particularly sensitive to intrusive enforcement, interpreting it as a betrayal of institutional trust. Resistant or disengaged taxpayers, by contrast, may be less affected by coercive measures, or even respond positively to stronger deterrence if it confirms their expectations regarding institutional hostility. Game-playing taxpayers may instead interpret enforcement as part of a strategic environment, adapting their behavior without significant moral disengagement.

Integrating these behavioral profiles with the Slippery Slope Framework allows for more precise and context-sensitive predictions. At the same time, crowding-out effects are more likely to emerge in historically high-trust environments, where excessive or poorly calibrated enforcement risks undermining voluntary compliance. Conversely, in lower-trust contexts, credible deterrence may play a more central stabilizing role within the compliance climate.

This ecosystemic view suggests that compliance cannot be fully understood as a simple additive function. A taxpayer's behavior is not simply the sum of deterrence and intrinsic motivation, but the result of interactions between personal dispositions, institutional signals, and social feedback. This perspective invites a shift from static policy levers to adaptive, feedback-sensitive governance.

One of the most significant insights emerging from this integrated perspective is what can be described as a behavioral policy paradox. Interventions designed to increase compliance through stronger enforcement may, under certain conditions, weaken the very motivational foundations that sustain it. This occurs when enforcement is perceived as excessive, misaligned with prevailing norms, or indicative of institutional mistrust, thereby altering the relational equilibrium between taxpayers and authorities.

Rather than implying a wholesale rejection of enforcement, this paradox highlights the importance of calibration. Effective policy design requires not the maximization of deterrence, but a context-sensitive balance between enforcement capacity and institutional legitimacy. In this sense, the impact of enforcement depends not only on its intensity, but also on how it is perceived, communicated, and embedded within broader institutional relationships.

This approach moves beyond the binary of "carrots vs. sticks" and toward a relational understanding of compliance, in which the interaction between taxpayers and institutions becomes central. Enforcement remains necessary, but its effectiveness depends increasingly on the legitimacy of the institutional environment in which it operates.

Ultimately, integrating behavioral frameworks into tax policy is not about replacing enforcement with trust, but about understanding how the two interact over time. Tax systems are more likely to remain stable and resilient when institutional behavior reinforces, rather than erodes, intrinsic motivations and perceptions of fairness.

2.4.6 Strategic Reflections and Future Directions

The integration of behavioral frameworks into tax compliance research has transformed our understanding of why people pay taxes. Yet, the real challenge lies not in accumulating more models, but in reframing how we think about compliance itself.

In fact, behavioral insights are increasingly being incorporated into tax administration across different jurisdictions through digital governance, policy experimentation, and behavioral segmentation strategies.

Alongside digitalization, governments have increasingly experimented with behavioral interventions designed to influence compliance indirectly. Nudging strategies, such as messages emphasizing peer compliance or highlighting the public benefits financed through taxation, have been implemented in several countries with measurable, though often context-dependent and modest, effects on taxpayer behavior (Hallsworth et al. 2014). Participatory budgeting initiatives and transparency platforms, adopted in various European contexts, further reinforce perceptions of reciprocity and fairness by making public expenditure more visible and accessible to citizens (Allegretti et al. 2021; Manes-Rossi et al. 2023). These initiatives demonstrate that behavioral interventions can be relatively low-cost, scalable, and legitimacy-enhancing, particularly when tailored to local contexts and supported by credible institutions.

One important implication of these behavioral approaches concerns the meso-level environments where fiscal norms are actively transmitted and reinforced. In many contemporary tax systems, the relationship between taxpayers and tax authorities is not direct, but is mediated by accountants, tax advisors, compliance professionals, and fiscal assistance agencies. These actors do not merely perform a technical support function; they also shape perceptions of risk, fairness, and institutional legitimacy. In this sense, intermediaries operate as genuine "institutional translators," filtering regulatory complexity and influencing how tax obligations are interpreted and internalized.

The behavioral impact of intermediaries, however, may evolve in different directions. In some contexts, they facilitate compliance by reducing uncertainty, cognitive costs, and unintentional errors. In others, particularly within complex or unstable regulatory environments, they may contribute to the diffusion of aggressive avoidance practices, normalizing tax minimization strategies and reinforcing a view of taxation as a purely technical and strategic exercise. Tax compliance therefore emerges not only from the interaction between taxpayers and the state, but also from the professional norms, economic incentives, and interpretive cultures that characterize broader tax intermediation ecosystems.

Another promising direction concerns the concept of behavioral resilience, namely the capacity of tax systems to preserve voluntary compliance during periods of institutional stress, economic crisis, or political instability. In lower-trust settings, as documented in cross-country analyses of tax morale (Torgler 2007), macro-level shocks can easily deplete the structural capital of compliance. Future research should therefore investigate how trust, motivational postures, and social norms react to external shocks and how digital platforms, which increasingly mediate the everyday interactions between taxpayers and the state, can be leveraged to sustain institutional credibility during fiscal crises.

Traditional indicators such as audit rates or revenue performance capture only part of this process. Behavioral resilience instead focuses on how trust, motivational postures, and social norms react to external shocks and how quickly they can recover once damaged.

This perspective suggests the need for more dynamic indicators capable of capturing the stability of compliance regimes over time. Concepts such as trust elasticity, norm volatility, or compliance inertia may help policymakers better understand the fragility or persistence of voluntary cooperation under changing institutional conditions.

More broadly, behavioral approaches imply that tax systems should be evaluated not only according to efficiency or equity criteria, but also according to their capacity to sustain legitimacy, transparency, and civic trust. Fiscal governance is therefore not simply a matter of maximizing revenue collection, but also of maintaining the institutional conditions that support long-term cooperation between citizens and the state.

In conclusion, behavioral frameworks do more than refine traditional theories of tax compliance. They suggest a broader transformation in how fiscal systems are understood and governed, emphasizing that stable and resilient compliance depends not only on enforcement capacity, but also on the quality of institutional relationships, perceptions of fairness, and the long-term credibility of public institutions.

2.5 Institutional Signals

2.5.1 Introduction: Rethinking Compliance Through Interaction

The previous sections have shown that tax compliance emerges from the interaction between external incentives and intrinsic motivations. Behavioral frameworks such as Motivational Postures, the Slippery Slope Framework, and crowding-out effects illustrate how enforcement, trust, legitimacy, and social norms jointly shape taxpayer behavior. Yet these approaches also point toward a broader question: how do citizens evaluate the relationship between what they contribute and what they receive from the state?

From this perspective, fiscal systems can generate both virtuous and vicious dynamics. When taxation is associated with visible public benefits, fair procedures, and credible institutions, voluntary cooperation may be reinforced. Conversely, when institutional signals undermine perceptions of fairness, reciprocity, or enforcement credibility, trust and tax morale may deteriorate. The following sections explore these two dimensions of fiscal exchange, examining both the conditions that strengthen voluntary compliance and the institutional mechanisms that may weaken it over time.

2.5.2 Tax Exchange and the Provision of Public Goods: Between Fairness and Enforcement

Let us begin with a deceptively simple question: *In what kind of State would we prefer to live?* One that relies on audits, penalties, and the threat of sanctions to compel us to pay taxes? Or one that appeals to our sense of fairness, civic duty, and shared responsibility?

Most of us would instinctively choose the second: a society where compliance is voluntary, trust in institutions is high, and taxation is perceived as a legitimate contribution to the common good. But what if the question were framed differently: *In what kind of State would we prefer to live, knowing that the money collected through taxation is used to provide essential public goods (like justice, healthcare, education, clean streets, functioning infrastructure) and local services (like waste collection and public lighting)?*

Suddenly, the answer becomes less obvious. The provision of public goods introduces a layer of complexity that challenges the ideal of purely voluntary compliance. It forces us to confront the tension between individual preferences and collective needs, between intrinsic motivations and the necessity of enforcement.

This tension is captured by the concept of tax exchange, to be intended as the perceived fairness and utility of public goods relative to the taxes paid. When taxpayers believe that their contributions are used efficiently and equitably, intrinsic motivation is strengthened. Compliance becomes not just a legal obligation, but a civic act. Conversely, when public spending is opaque, wasteful, or corrupt, trust erodes, and enforcement becomes the dominant driver of compliance.

The literature on tax exchange and public goods provision is both rich and evolving. Bordignon (1993) laid the groundwork by linking fairness perceptions to compliance behavior. More recently, D'Agostino et al. (2021) provided empirical evidence from Italian provinces showing that higher public spending, especially when perceived as efficient, reduces tax evasion. Their findings highlight the importance of both the quantity and quality of public goods in shaping taxpayer behavior.

Importantly, exchange theory occupies a conceptual space that bridges external incentives and intrinsic motivations. On one hand, the provision of public goods by the state can be interpreted as an external incentive, like an institutional signal that taxes are reciprocated with tangible benefits. On the other hand, this provision can activate intrinsic motivations, such as civic pride, trust, and moral obligation. In this sense, the tax exchange is not merely a transactional mechanism but a psychological and normative trigger that fosters voluntary compliance.

A further point concerns the distinction between quantity and quality: taxpayers may react not only to the quantity of public expenditure, but also to the perceived quality of the goods and services provided. High levels of public spending do not necessarily strengthen compliance if public services are perceived as inefficient or poorly managed. This issue is particularly relevant in sectors such as healthcare and education, where qualitative dimensions often matter as much as formal availability. However, the quality of public goods is not always easily observable by taxpayers, generating informational asymmetries that may weaken reciprocal expectations and institutional credibility. Here again, media play a critical role.

By reporting on the state of public infrastructure, healthcare, education, and local services, media shape public perceptions of whether the fiscal exchange is equitable or exploitative. Positive coverage can reinforce trust and intrinsic motivation; negative coverage may fuel skepticism and resistance (Kirchler 2007; Prichard 2015).

Thus, the media function as both amplifiers and filters of institutional signals. They mediate the relationship between taxpayers and the state, influencing how public goods are perceived and how compliance norms are internalized. In contexts where institutional trust is fragile, strategic media engagement (through transparency dashboards, participatory reporting, and civic journalism) can help restore legitimacy and strengthen the fiscal contract.

Experimental studies reinforce this view. Carrillo et al. (2021) demonstrate that improvements in local public services increase property tax compliance in Latin America. Montenbruck (2025) shows that simply informing citizens about public service provision can raise compliance by up to 20% in low-capacity states.

Other contributions, such as Hsu (2008) and Hokamp and Seibold (2014), explore the behavioral feedback between public goods and tax morale, using experimental and agent-based models to show how visible improvements in services can reduce evasion even among self-interested taxpayers.

Moreover, tax exchange can mediate the relationship between enforcement and motivation. When enforcement is paired with visible, high-quality public spending, it signals legitimacy and reinforces intrinsic motivation. Digital dashboards in Estonia and Singapore, for example, allow taxpayers to see how their contributions fund tangible outcomes, enhancing both trust and compliance. In such contexts, enforcement does not crowd out motivation; rather it complements it.

Conversely, in low-trust environments, enforcement may be necessary to sustain compliance, but it cannot substitute for legitimacy. Brazil and parts of Southern Europe illustrate how weak public services and perceived unfairness undermine intrinsic motivation, forcing governments to rely on costly and often ineffective deterrence.

In sum, the quality of the tax exchange, and not just the presence of enforcement or the strength of tax morale, determines the sustainability of compliance. A well-designed fiscal system aligns extrinsic and intrinsic motivations, creating a virtuous cycle in which public goods reinforce trust, and trust reduces the need for coercion. This insight has profound implications for policy design, especially in an era of fiscal stress and democratic fragility.

In a simple model presented in Chapter 4, these informational and qualitative dimensions of public goods provision may also shape taxpayers' strategic behavior. In particular, transparency and taxpayers' ability to evaluate public expenditure quality may influence the sustainability of different compliance equilibria.

2.5.3 *Tax Amnesties: Between Incentive and Institutional Signals*

Tax amnesties occupy a controversial and strategically ambiguous position within the landscape of fiscal policy instruments. They are typically framed as pragmatic tools to recover revenue, reduce litigation, and re-integrate noncompliant taxpayers into the formal system. Yet, their behavioral and institutional implications go far beyond short-term fiscal gains. Positioned between deterrence and legitimacy, amnesties challenge the dichotomy between external incentives and intrinsic motivations, and force us to confront the political economy of compliance.

From a policy design perspective, tax amnesties are external incentives: they offer a temporary relaxation of enforcement in exchange for voluntary disclosure and payment. They reduce the expected cost of evasion by allowing taxpayers to regularize past behavior without facing full penalties. In this sense, they operate within the logic of deterrence, albeit in a softened and conditional form. However, unlike audits or fines, amnesties also send a powerful institutional signal. They communicate something about the state's priorities, its capacity to enforce rules, and its willingness to compromise. This signal can either reinforce or undermine the psychological contract between citizens and institutions.

The economic literature has long debated the effectiveness of tax amnesties. Alm et al. (1990) showed that amnesties can increase short-term compliance, especially when followed by credible enforcement. Baer and Le Borgne (2008), in their IMF study, highlighted the short-term fiscal benefits that tax amnesties may generate, while warning against their repeated use and their potential long-term effects on compliance. Luitel and Sobel (2007) found that frequent amnesties create expectations of future leniency, thereby reducing long-term compliance. More broadly, the tax compliance literature has consistently emphasized the importance of enforcement credibility and taxpayer expectations in shaping long-term compliance behavior (Andreoni et al. 1998).

Psychological and behavioral research adds further nuance. Torgler and Schaltegger (2005) argue that amnesties can crowd out intrinsic motivations by weakening the moral stigma associated with evasion. Feld and Frey (2007) suggest that amnesties may violate the implicit psychological tax contract, especially if perceived as unfair by compliant taxpayers. Kirchler (2007) highlights the role of trust and legitimacy in shaping taxpayer responses to amnesties, noting that in low-trust environments, amnesties may reinforce cynicism and strategic evasion.

Empirical evidence confirms this ambivalence. Italy has implemented over a dozen tax amnesties since the 1980s, often justified by the need to recover revenue and reduce judicial backlog. Recent evidence from Angeli et al. (2023) indicates that the 2016–2019 Italian tax amnesty yielded limited revenue recovery and may have increased the likelihood of future noncompliance. Argentina's 2016 "blanqueo" program disclosed assets worth 21% of GDP, significantly expanding the wealth tax base and improving progressivity (Londoño-Vélez and Tortarolo 2022). Indonesia's 2016–17 amnesty raised substantial revenue and broadened the tax base, though concerns remain about its long-term impact on compliance (Hajawiyah et al. 2021).

Politically, tax amnesties are more frequently used by governments facing fiscal stress, electoral pressure, or institutional fragility. Populist and clientelist regimes tend to favor amnesties to signal leniency and reward strategic evasion. In contrast, high-trust democracies with strong enforcement institutions use amnesties sparingly and often frame them as exceptional measures tied to broader reforms. The political use of amnesties thus reflects deeper tensions between rule-based governance and discretionary power.

In the short term, amnesties can be effective in recovering revenue and reducing administrative burden. They offer a pragmatic solution to systemic noncompliance and can serve as a reset mechanism. But in the long term, their effects are more problematic. They may erode tax morale, distort expectations, and undermine the credibility of enforcement. They can also create horizontal inequity, by rewarding evaders and penalizing honest taxpayers. Thus, by signaling that evasion is ultimately negotiable, amnesties weaken the normative foundations of voluntary compliance.

In the framework developed in this chapter, tax amnesties exemplify the tension between strategic incentives and institutional legitimacy. They are not neutral tools, but behavioral interventions with deep normative consequences. Their design, framing, and sequencing matter. A well-designed amnesty, embedded into a broader reform and followed by credible enforcement, may enhance compliance. A poorly designed or politically motivated amnesty may do the opposite.

Future research should explore the conditions under which amnesties reinforce or undermine compliance, and how they interact with taxpayer psychology, institutional trust, and political context. What is clear is that tax amnesties are not just fiscal instruments, but also strategic signals. And like all signals, their meaning depends on the context in which they are sent and the expectations they generate.

2.6 Conclusion

Tax compliance is often presented as a technical issue centered on audits, penalties, and enforcement capacity. Yet the analysis developed throughout this chapter suggests that compliance is also deeply shaped by legitimacy, institutional quality, social norms, and perceptions of fairness. Taxpayer behavior emerges from the interaction between external incentives and intrinsic motivations, and this interaction is neither linear nor stable across contexts.

The chapter has shown that deterrence remains necessary, but insufficient on its own. Enforcement can sustain compliance when it is perceived as proportionate, transparent, and legitimate; however, when experienced as arbitrary or excessively coercive, it may undermine trust and weaken voluntary cooperation. At the same time, intrinsic motivations such as tax morale, civic duty, and social norms cannot be treated as fixed cultural traits. They evolve through repeated interactions between citizens and institutions, and are strongly influenced by public governance, institutional credibility, and the perceived fairness of the fiscal exchange.

Behavioral approaches help illuminate these dynamics by emphasizing the relational and adaptive nature of compliance. Motivational Postures, the Slippery Slope Framework, crowding-out effects, and exchange theory each contribute to a broader understanding of how taxpayers interpret institutional behavior and how compliance regimes emerge, stabilize, or deteriorate over time. These perspectives suggest that effective tax systems depend not only on enforcement capacity, but also on the ability of institutions to maintain trust, transparency, and reciprocal legitimacy.

This insight opens several important questions for future research and policy design. How do motivational postures evolve in response to political or economic shocks? What institutional conditions strengthen behavioral resilience and preserve voluntary cooperation during periods of crisis? To what extent can digital governance, participatory mechanisms, and transparency tools reinforce long-term tax morale? And how can policymakers balance enforcement credibility with the need to preserve trust and civic engagement?

Ultimately, the challenge for modern tax systems is not simply to maximize compliance in the short run, but to sustain it over time without eroding the social and institutional foundations on which it depends. In this sense, tax compliance should not be understood merely as a reaction to coercion or incentives, but as part of a broader relationship between citizens and public institutions, shaped by reciprocity, legitimacy, and collective expectations.

References

Allegretti, G., Bassoli, M. & Colavolpe, G. (2021). On the Verge of Institutionalisation? Participatory Budgeting Evidence in Five Italian Regions. *Financial Journal* 13(2), 25–45.

Allingham, M. G. & Sandmo, A. (1972). Income Tax Evasion: A Theoretical Analysis. *Journal of Public Economics* 1(3–4), 323–338.

Alm, J., McClelland, G. H. and Schulze, W. D. (1992). Why Do People Pay Taxes? *Journal of Public Economics* 48(1), 21–38.

Alm, J., McKee, M., & Beck, W. (1990). Amazing Grace: Tax Amnesties and Compliance. *National Tax Journal* 43(1), 23–37.

Alm, J. & Torgler, B. (2006). Culture Differences and Tax Morale in the United States and Europe. *Journal of Economic Psychology* 27(2), 224–246.

Andreoni, J., Erard, B. & Feinstein, J. (1998). Tax Compliance. *Journal of Economic Literature*, 36(2), 818–860.

Angeli, A., Lattarulo, P., Palmieri, E. & Pazienza, M. G. (2023). Tax Evasion and Tax Amnesties in Regional Taxation. *Economia Politica* 40(2), 343–369.

Antinyan, A. & Asatryan, Z. (2025). Nudging for Tax Compliance: A Meta-Analysis. *The Economic Journal* 135(668), 1033–1068.

Baer, K. & Le Borgne, E. (2008). *Tax Amnesties: Theory, Trends, and some Alternatives*. Washington, DC: International Monetary Fund.

Bordignon, M. (1993). A Fairness Approach to Income Tax Evasion. *Journal of Public Economics* 52(3), 345–362.

Braithwaite, V. (2003). *Taxing Democracy: Understanding Tax Avoidance and Evasion*. Ashgate.

Carrillo, P. E., Castro, E. & Scartascini, C. (2021). Public Good Provision and Property Tax Compliance: Evidence from a Natural Experiment. *Journal of Public Economics* 198, 104422.

D'Agostino, E., De Benedetto, M.A. & Sobbrio, G. (2021). Tax Evasion and Government Size: Evidence from Italian Provinces. *Economia Politica* 38(3), 1149–1187.

Deparade, D., Jarmolinski, L., Mohr, P. N. C. (2025). Behavioral Interventions, Tax Compliance and Consequences on Inequality. *School of Business and Economics Discussion Paper 2025/4, Freie Universität Berlin.*

Feld, L. P. & Frey, B. S. (2007). Tax Compliance as the Result of a Psychological Tax Contract: The Role of Incentives and Responsive Regulation. *Law & Policy* 29(1), 102–120.

Fellner, G., Sausgruber, R. & Traxler, C. (2013). Testing Enforcement Strategies in the Field: Threat, Moral Appeal and Social Information. *Journal of the European Economic Association* 11(3), 634–660.

Fortin, B., Lacroix, G. & Villeval, M. C. (2007). Tax Evasion and Social Interactions. *Journal of Public Economics* 91(11–12), 2089–2112.

Frey, B. S. (1997). *Not Just for the Money: An Economic Theory of Personal Motivation.* Cheltenham, UK: Edward Elgar Publishing.

Frey, B. S. & Jegen, R. (2001). Motivation Crowding Theory. *Journal of Economic Surveys* 15(5), 589–611.

Frey, B. S. & Torgler, B. (2007). Tax Morale and Conditional Cooperation. *Journal of Comparative Economics* 35(1), 136–159.

Friedland, N., Maital, S. & Rutenberg, A. (1978). A Simulation Study on Income Tax Evasion. *Journal of Public Economics* 10, 107–116.

Hajawiyah, A., Suryarini, T., Kiswanto & Tarmudji, T. (2021). Analysis of a Tax Amnesty's Effectiveness in Indonesia. *Journal of International Accounting, Auditing and Taxation* 44, 100415.

Hallsworth, M., List, J. A., Metcalfe, R. D. & Vlaev, I. (2014). The Behavioralist as Tax Collector: Using Natural Field Experiments to Enhance Tax Compliance. *Journal of Public Economics* 117, 14–25.

Hanlon, A. & Heitzman, S. (2010). A Review of Tax Research. *Journal of Accounting and Economics* 50(2-3), 127–178.

Hokamp, S. & Seibold, G. (2014). Tax Compliance and Public Goods Provision: An Agent-Based Econophysics Approach. *Central European Journal of Economic Modelling and Econometrics* 6(4), 217–236.

Hsu, L.-C. (2008). Experimental evidence on tax compliance and voluntary public good provision. *National Tax Journal, 61*(2), 205–223.

Kirchler, E. (2007). *The Economic Psychology of Tax Behaviour.* Cambridge University Press.

Kirchler, E., Hoelzl, E. & Wahl, I. (2008). Enforced versus Coluntary Tax Compliance: The "Slippery Slope" Framework. *Journal of Economic Psychology* 29(2), 210–225.

Londoño-Vélez, J. & Tortarolo, D. (2022). *Revealing 21 percent of GDP in Hidden Assets: Evidence from Argentina's Tax Amnesties.* WIDER Working Paper 2022/103. United Nations University.

Luitel, H. S. & Sobel, R. S. (2007). The Revenue Impact of Repeated Tax Amnesties. *Public Budgeting and Finance* 27(3), 19–38.

Luttmer, E. F. P. & Singhal, M. (2014). Tax Morale. *Journal of Economic Perspectives* 28(4), 149–168.

Manes-Rossi, F., Brusca, I., Levy Orelli, R., Lorson, P. C. & Hausteind, E. (2023). Features and Drivers of Citizen Participation: Insights from Participatory Budgeting in three European Cities. *Public Management Review* 25(2), 201–223.

Montenbruck, L. (2025). Fiscal Exchange and Tax Compliance: Strengthening the Social Contract under Low State Capacity. CRC TR 224 Discussion Paper Series crctr 224_2025_620, University of Bonn and University of Mannheim, Germany.

OECD (2021). *Tax Administration 2021: Comparative Information on OECD and Other Advanced and Emerging Economies.* OECD Publishing.

Prichard, W. (2015). *Taxation, Responsiveness and Accountability in sub-Saharan Africa: The Dynamics of Tax Bargaining.* Cambridge University Press.

Richardson, G. (2006). Determinants of Tax Evasion: A Cross-Country Analysis. *Journal of International Accounting, Auditing and Taxation* 15(2), 150–169.

Slemrod, J. (2007). Cheating Ourselves: The Economics of Tax Evasion. *Journal of Economic Perspectives* 21(1), 25–48.

Slemrod, J., Blumenthal, M. & Christian, C. (2001). Taxpayer Response to an Increased Probability of Audit: Evidence from a Controlled Experiment in Minnesota. *Journal of Public Economics*, 79(3), 455–483.

Slemrod, J. & Yitzhaki, S. (2002). Tax Avoidance, Evasion, and Administration. In A. J. Auerbach & M. Feldstein (Eds.), *Handbook of Public Economics*, Vol. 3 (pp. 1423–1470). Amsterdam: Elsevier.

Torgler, B. (2007). *Tax Compliance and Tax Morale: A Theoretical and Empirical Analysis.* Edward Elgar Publishing.

Torgler, B. & Schaltegger, C. A. (2005). Tax Amnesties and Political Participation. *Public Finance Review* 33(3), 403–431.

Tyler, T. R. (1990). *Why People Obey the Law.* Yale University Press.

Wahl, I., Kastlunger, B. & Kirchler, E. (2010). Trust in Authorities and Power to Enforce Tax Compliance: An Empirical Analysis of the "Slippery Slope Framework". *Law & Policy* 32(4), 383–406.

CHAPTER 3

Measuring Tax Evasion

Abstract This chapter addresses the methodological paradox of quantifying a hidden phenomenon. It critically examines the tax gap as the dominant proxy, highlighting its conceptual ambiguities and normative implications. The discussion covers audit-based methods, macroeconomic models, and emerging computational approaches, emphasizing their assumptions and limitations. Comparative analysis reveals the challenges of cross-country benchmarking, shaped by legal definitions, administrative capacity, and political narratives. The chapter introduces the concept of plausibility over precision, advocating humility in measurement and transparency in interpretation. A novel contribution is the proposal to integrate motivational dimensions into evasion metrics, moving beyond static discrepancies toward relational indicators. This behavioral approach aligns measurement with the book's normative vision: that compliance is not merely a technical outcome but a reflection of institutional legitimacy and civic engagement.

Keywords Tax gap • Methodological uncertainty • Audit-based estimation • Macro-level models • Behavioral measurement

E. D'Agostino, *The Determinants of Tax Evasion*, Palgrave Studies in Institutions, Economics and Law,
https://doi.org/10.1007/978-3-032-21897-1_3

3.1 Measuring the Unmeasurable? A Methodological Prelude

This chapter is entirely devoted to the methodological challenges and tools for measuring tax evasion. I begin by tracing a threefold analytical path: why measurement matters, why it is inherently imperfect, and why acknowledging its limitations is vital for sound policy design. These questions guide the exploration of the conceptual, methodological, and policy dimensions of tax evasion measurement.

Tax evasion is, by definition, an act of concealment. It thrives in the shadows of economic activity, eluding detection and defying quantification. Yet, paradoxically, measuring it is indispensable because without measurement tax evasion remains a rhetorical construct: it is politically charged, normatively contested, and empirically vague. Therefore, measurement becomes essential because it renders a hidden phenomenon into a policy-relevant object of analysis. It allows us to estimate revenue losses, identify behavioral patterns, and evaluate enforcement strategies. In doing so, it does not merely reveal tax evasion; it shapes how the phenomenon is defined and interpreted. For this reason, measuring tax evasion is necessarily based on approximation, given the concealed nature of the phenomenon itself (Richupan 1984; Slemrod 2007).

But this measurement is inherently imperfect. Unlike more directly measurable macroeconomic variables (such as GDP, inflation, or unemployment), tax evasion resists direct observation. It is not declared, not recorded, and often deliberately distorted. The tools employed (random audits, discrepancy analysis, macroeconomic modeling, and survey-based inference) are all proxies. They rely on assumptions, suffer from selection biases, and often produce divergent results. Measuring tax evasion is therefore inherently probabilistic and assumption-driven.

Acknowledging these limitations should not be regarded as a weakness, but rather as a methodological necessity. Because tax evasion estimates are inherently uncertain, sound policy design must remain grounded in realism rather than in an illusion of precision. Excessive confidence in incomplete or fragile data may lead to misallocated resources, ineffective deterrence strategies, and unintended institutional consequences. By contrast, recognizing the uncertainty embedded in tax evasion measurement encourages greater methodological humility and supports more adaptive forms of policymaking. In this sense, the objective of measurement shifts from the pursuit of exact precision toward the construction of plausible and context-sensitive interpretative frameworks.

The following sections examine the problem of measuring tax evasion from multiple methodological and conceptual perspectives. The chapter explores the ambiguities surrounding the definition of tax evasion, the limitations of existing estimation techniques, and the interpretative challenges associated with hidden economic behavior. Particular attention is devoted to the relationship between measurement, institutional credibility, and public narratives, emphasizing that tax evasion estimates are not merely technical outputs, but also instruments that shape policy debates, perceptions of legitimacy, and fiscal governance strategies.

3.2 Definitional and Operational Issues

While the conceptual boundaries of tax evasion have been extensively discussed in Chapter 1, through economic, legal, political, sociological, and psychological lenses, this section shifts the focus toward its operationalization in empirical research. It explores how tax evasion is defined and quantified in practice, with attention to the methodological ambiguities that complicate its measurement.

3.2.1 From Concept to Quantification: The Tax Gap

One of the most widely used operational proxies for tax non-compliance, and indirectly for tax evasion, is the tax gap, defined as the difference between the tax that should be collected under full compliance and the amount actually collected. This concept, popularized by tax administrations such as the U.S. Internal Revenue Service (IRS) and the UK's HM Revenue and Customs (HMRC), serves as a benchmark for estimating the scale of noncompliance. It encompasses various forms of evasion, including underreporting of income, non-filing, and underpayment, and is often disaggregated by tax type (examples are income tax or VAT) and taxpayer category.

Despite its intuitive appeal, the tax gap is not a direct measure of evasion but a construct derived from a combination of audit data, statistical models, and assumptions about taxpayer behavior. As such, it is subject to significant uncertainty. For instance, the IRS's methodology relies on random audits and extrapolations that may not capture all forms of systematic evasion (Slemrod 2007). Moreover, the tax gap does not distinguish between intentional evasion and errors; nor can it always clearly distinguish legal tax avoidance strategies from more aggressive forms of noncompliance, further complicating the interpretation of tax gap estimates.

3.2.2 *Conceptual Ambiguities and Measurement Implications*

The operationalization of tax evasion is fraught with conceptual ambiguities that affect both the validity and comparability of empirical estimates. First, the boundary between evasion and avoidance presents a profound challenge that is fundamentally normative and legal rather than merely statistical (see Section 1.5). While avoidance is formally permissible under the letter of the law, aggressive tax planning increasingly leverages statutory loopholes in ways that violate the spirit of the legislation. In modern fiscal governance, this tension increasingly emerges in the context of anti-avoidance doctrines and regulatory frameworks aimed at addressing tax avoidance and non-compliance (OECD 2017). This shifting legal landscape complicates the construction of reliable indicators; what firms initially structure as legitimate tax planning may later be challenged by tax authorities or courts as abusive or noncompliant arrangements, leading to persistent systemic misclassification and undermining the comparative validity of tax gap estimates.

Second, the notion of "potential tax liability" used in tax gap calculations is itself highly contestable from both an economic and sociological perspective. It fundamentally depends on idealized assumptions about full compliance, which vary across institutional contexts and over time. For example, in economies characterized by structural informal sectors or limited administrative capacity, treating the baseline for "full compliance" as a universal standard is inherently speculative and normative (Schneider and Enste 2000). This raises fundamental questions about the normative dimension of measurement: what is quantified as evasion is not merely a technical residual, but a reflection of how state authority and fiscal boundaries are legally and socially constructed.

Third, cross-country comparisons are particularly problematic. Differences in tax systems, enforcement regimes, and data availability mean that tax gap estimates are rarely fully standardized. As noted by Cobham and Janský (2018), international efforts to estimate cross-border tax avoidance and profit shifting, particularly within the broader BEPS debate, continue to face significant methodological and data-related challenges that complicate comparability across jurisdictions.

These conceptual ambiguities are not merely academic; they have direct normative consequences. When the boundary between evasion and avoidance is blurred, policymakers may struggle to justify enforcement actions or to design equitable tax reforms. Moreover, if measurement tools fail to distinguish between intentional fraud and honest error, enforcement strategies risk being perceived as unjust, potentially undermining taxpayer trust. Thus, the operationalization of evasion is not only a technical challenge but also a normative one, shaping the legitimacy, proportionality, and targeting of fiscal interventions.

3.3 Methodological Challenges

As stated earlier, measuring tax evasion is not merely a technical exercise; it is a methodological endeavor fraught with epistemic uncertainty, data limitations, and conceptual ambiguity. This section outlines the principal challenges that researchers face when attempting to quantify a phenomenon that is, by design, hidden from view.

As already highlighted, tax evasion is an act of deliberate concealment. Unlike observable economic behaviors, it leaves no fully reliable or complete trace in administrative records. As Richupan (1984) noted, the illegal nature of evasion necessitates secrecy, making direct measurement virtually impossible. Instead, researchers must rely on indirect indicators, such as discrepancies between reported and undeclared income, or between macroeconomic aggregates and tax receipts, which are themselves subject to interpretation and error.

This reliance on indirect evidence introduces a fundamental epistemological asymmetry: we can observe declared compliance, but we infer evasion. Consequently, any estimate of tax evasion is contingent on the assumptions embedded in the chosen methodology.

3.3.1 Selection Bias and Data Limitations

One of the most pervasive challenges in empirical studies of tax evasion is selection bias. Many audit-based approaches, such as those used by the IRS and other tax authorities, tend to focus on high-risk taxpayers, leading to non-random samples. Random audit programs were introduced precisely to mitigate this representativeness problem.

However, as demonstrated by Guyton et al. (2023), even random audits may fail to capture sophisticated forms of evasion, such as offshore accounts and complex pass-through business structures, especially among high-income individuals.

Moreover, the data available to researchers are often incomplete, outdated, or restricted due to confidentiality concerns. Even when microdata are accessible, they may lack the granularity needed to detect nuanced forms of noncompliance. The problem is compounded in countries with limited administrative capacity, where tax records may be unreliable or inconsistently maintained.

3.3.2 Assumptions in Estimation Models

All estimation techniques, whether econometric, simulation-based, or behavioral, rely on assumptions about taxpayer behavior, enforcement effectiveness, and the structure of the tax system. For instance, detection-controlled econometric models developed in the tax compliance literature explicitly account for imperfect detection by modeling the relationship between evasion and audit outcomes. Feinstein (1991), in particular, allows detection probabilities to vary systematically with factors such as return complexity and examiner-specific characteristics. While this approach improves upon naïve audit extrapolation, it remains sensitive to parametric assumptions and identification problems related to unobserved heterogeneity and endogenous detection.

From this perspective, agent-based models (ABMs) offer a promising alternative by simulating heterogeneous taxpayer behavior under varying institutional conditions. However, these models require extensive calibration and validation, and their results are often highly sensitive to parameterization (see Section 3.4.3).

3.3.3 Cross-Country Comparability: A Persistent Challenge

Comparing tax evasion across countries is a tempting but methodologically fraught endeavor. While international organizations such as the OECD, IMF, and the EU Tax Observatory have made significant strides in harmonizing tax data and promoting transparency, substantial obstacles remain in achieving meaningful comparability.

One of the primary challenges lies in the heterogeneity of tax systems. As already noted, countries differ not only in their tax rates and structures but also in their legal definitions of taxable income, exemptions, and enforcement mechanisms. For instance, what constitutes "evasion" in one jurisdiction may be classified as "avoidance" or even legal tax planning in another. This definitional fluidity undermines the comparability of tax gap estimates and complicates cross-national benchmarking.

In addition, administrative capacity plays a crucial role in shaping the reliability of tax evasion estimates. High-income countries with robust tax administrations, such as the U.S., the UK, and Scandinavian nations, can produce detailed audit data and conduct randomized compliance studies. In contrast, low- and middle-income countries often lack the infrastructure to collect and process granular tax data, leading to reliance on macro-level proxies or outdated surveys, as highlighted in the empirical literature on developing-country tax capacity.

Even when such data are available, differences in reporting standards, such as those found in Country-by-Country Reports (CbCRs), can introduce inconsistencies. A recent benchmarking study by the EU Tax Observatory found that while most CbCR data appear broadly consistent with consolidated financial statements, definitional discrepancies and scope limitations still persist across reporting practices (Aliprandi and von Zedlitz 2023).

Another aspect to keep in mind is that countries employ a wide range of methodologies to estimate their tax gaps, including bottom-up approaches based on audit data and top-down models using national accounts. The IMF's RA-GAP program, for example, has examined bottom-up approaches across different country contexts, emphasizing how differences in extimation techniques, data availability, and coverage may complicate direct cross-country comparisons (Barra et al. 2023).

Even within the OECD member countries, tax gap estimates vary significantly in both scope and interpretation, reflecting different institutional understandings of noncompliance. The UK's HMRC, for example, incorporates behavioral categories such as "failure to take reasonable care" and "legal interpretation" into its estimates, whereas the U.S. IRS adopts a comparatively narrower focus centered primarily on underreporting and non-filing (HM Revenue and Customs 2025). As detailed in HMRC's methodological annex, these behavioral dimensions are explicitly integrated into the official estimation framework. Such differences illustrate how even advanced tax administrations operationalize noncompliance through partially distinct conceptual and methodological lenses, thereby further complicating international benchmarking exercises.

Despite these challenges, several initiatives offer hope for improved comparability. The OECD/G20 Inclusive Framework on BEPS has introduced standardized reporting requirements and minimum tax thresholds, while the EU Tax Observatory continues to refine cross-country datasets and promote methodological transparency (EU Tax Observatory 2025).

However, as broader debates on comparability in supranational fiscal and legal frameworks suggest (Castagna 2023), even within supranational frameworks like the EU, WTO, and ISDS, the notion of "comparability" remains analytically and institutionally contested. True harmonization therefore requires not only methodological alignment, but also broader consensus on what constitutes legitimate and equitable taxation across jurisdictions.

3.4 Empirical Strategies and Tools

Quantifying tax evasion requires navigating a landscape of methodological trade-offs. Researchers and institutions have developed a range of empirical strategies—micro-level, macro-level, and increasingly, computational and data-driven approaches—to estimate the scope and dynamics of noncompliance. Each method offers distinct advantages and limitations, shaped by the nature of the data, the institutional context, and the underlying assumptions.

3.4.1 Micro-Level Approaches: Grounded but Partial

Micro-level approaches rely on individual-level data, typically drawn from tax audits, surveys, or behavioral experiments. Among these, audit-based estimation is the most widely used, particularly by tax authorities such as the IRS and HMRC. These studies compare reported income with income uncovered or adjusted during audits and extrapolate the findings to the broader taxpayer population.

The strength of audit-based methods lies in their concreteness: they provide the closest available direct evidence of evasion and allow for detailed analysis of taxpayer behavior.

However, as already discussed in Section 3.3, audit-based approaches present significant methodological limitations. Operational audits suffer from selection bias, as tax authorities naturally tend to focus on taxpayers considered high-risk. Even random audit programs, introduced to mitigate these distortions, remain vulnerable to detection failures. Recent literature shows that standard audits tend to systematically under-detect sophisticated forms of noncompliance at the top of the income distribution, such as offshore wealth and complex pass-through business structures (Guyton et al. 2023). Consequently, extrapolating raw audit findings to the general population requires increasingly fragile assumptions regarding both representativeness and uniform detection probabilities across different income brackets.

Survey-based methods offer a complementary perspective by capturing self-reported behavior and attitudes toward tax compliance. They are particularly useful for exploring the psychological and social dimensions of evasion, including perceptions of fairness, trust, and civic norms. However, these methods remain vulnerable to strategic misreporting and social desirability bias, especially when respondents fear repercussions or wish to present themselves in a favorable light.

To mitigate some of these limitations, the literature has increasingly relied on experimental designs, including randomized field interventions, which allow researchers to observe real-world behavioral responses to targeted treatments rather than relying exclusively on self-reported data.

While contemporary field experiments are often conducted on a massive scale, their main methodological limitations concern external validity and the typically short-term nature of behavioral nudges. As demonstrated by a comprehensive meta-analysis of tax field experiments (Antinyan and Asatryan, 2025), the effects of behavioral interventions vary across contexts and tend to be stronger in the short run, which may constrain the generalizability and long-term sustainability of such policies.

3.4.2 Macro-Level Approaches: Broad but Indirect

Macro-level approaches estimate tax evasion by analyzing discrepancies between aggregate economic indicators and tax revenues. These methods are especially valuable in contexts where microdata are scarce or unreliable. One classic technique is the currency demand approach, which infers the size of the shadow economy from excess cash holdings, under the strong and often contested assumption that undeclared transactions are more likely to be conducted in cash (Tanzi 1983).

Another widely used framework is the MIMIC model (Multiple Indicators Multiple Causes); however, the MIMIC framework does not capture tax evasion directly but rather treats the broader shadow economy as an unobservable latent variable (Schneider and Enste 2000).

While macro-level models offer broad coverage and can be applied across countries and over time, they are inherently indirect. Their validity depends heavily on the choice of variables, the specification of causal relationships, and the calibration of parameters.

Moreover, they often conflate tax evasion with other forms of informality and other non-observed economic activities, making it difficult to isolate the specific behaviors of interest. These models are best understood as heuristic tools; they are useful for identifying trends and magnitudes, but not for precise measurement.

3.4.3 *Computational and Data-Driven Approaches: Promising but Complex*

Recent advances in computational methods have opened new avenues for measuring tax evasion. Tax administrations increasingly employ big data analytics and machine learning to detect anomalies, flag suspicious behavior, and optimize audit selection. These techniques can process vast amounts of information, from bank records and e-invoices to transaction networks, allowing for something close to real-time monitoring and predictive modeling.

The strength of these approaches lies in their scalability and adaptability. Machine learning algorithms can potentially uncover patterns that are not easily detectable and may improve as new data become available. At the same time, however, these techniques raise broader concerns regarding transparency, accountability, and explainability in automated decision-making processes. In practice, many AI-based systems operate as partial "black boxes," making it difficult to fully understand how risk classifications are generated or to challenge them in legal contexts. Moreover, their effectiveness depends heavily on the quality and integration of underlying data systems, which vary considerably across jurisdictions (van Liebergen 2017).

Complementary to these data-driven tools, agent-based models (ABMs) represent a simulation-based strand of research driven by theoretical parameters. They simulate the behavior of heterogeneous taxpayers within virtual environments to observe how aggregate patterns of compliance emerge from individual behavior, incorporating factors such as risk aversion, social norms, and enforcement intensity. ABMs are particularly useful for exploring dynamic interactions and emergent phenomena, for example, how changes in audit probability affect compliance over time, or how peer behavior influences individual decisions (Hokamp et al. 2018, Vardavas et al. 2019). Yet, they require extensive calibration and are sensitive to initial conditions, which limits their generalizability. Their value lies more in scenario analysis than in empirical estimation.

3.5 Comparative Insights

Beyond the methodological comparability challenges discussed in Section 3.3.3, cross-country analysis also raises broader interpretative and institutional questions concerning the meaning and social construction of tax compliance itself.

What does it mean to compare tax evasion across countries? At first glance, it seems like a technical exercise, an effort to benchmark fiscal performance, identify best practices, and calibrate policy interventions. But beneath the surface, comparative analysis reveals a deeper tension: between the desire for universal metrics and the stubborn particularity of national contexts.

3.5.1 Beyond Metrics: Rethinking Comparison in Tax Evasion Research

Tax evasion is not a uniform phenomenon. It is shaped by legal definitions, administrative capacity, cultural norms, and political narratives. Just to provide an example, the tax gap in Denmark may reflect a fundamentally different reality than the same figure in Argentina or Nigeria. Even the act of measuring evasion is embedded in institutional storytelling: some countries invest heavily in quantification; others treat it as a political liability. Thus, when we compare, we are not merely juxtaposing numbers; rather, we are comparing what those numbers are interpreted to mean within their institutional contexts.

This raises an unconventional question: can tax evasion be meaningfully compared at all? Or are we chasing a mirage of methodological symmetry in a landscape of asymmetrical realities?

One underexplored dimension is trust. In high-trust societies, compliance may be driven less by deterrence and more by civic norms. In low-trust environments, evasion may be a natural response to perceived corruption or inefficiency. Wintrobe and Gërxhani (2004) suggest that differences in institutional trust, not just enforcement, explain cross-country variation in evasion rates. Yet, many standardized international benchmarking exercises and crude tax gap rankings often implicitly treat them as analytically comparable. By evaluating performance primarily through enforcement intensity and raw compliance percentages, such frameworks fail to account for the variance in underlying moral economies (in the sociological sense). Consequently, comparative analyses should rely on frameworks that integrate these qualitative dimensions into the empirical architecture, assessing the ethical underpinnings of compliance rather than just its compliance mechanics.

Another neglected aspect is narrative framing. In some countries, tax evasion is portrayed as a criminal act; in others, as a symptom of systemic failure. These framings shape public discourse, enforcement priorities, and even the willingness of researchers to engage with the topic. Tognato (2015) provides a robust cultural framework for these dynamics, demonstrating how tax compliance is deeply embedded in cultural codes and social meanings. In the Italian context, for instance, the historical perception of tax evaders as folk heroes resisting an oppressive state was powerfully reframed during the sovereign debt crisis, when political and media discourses increasingly cast noncompliance as an existential threat to national survival. Comparative studies that ignore these shifting discursive layers risk privileging technical equivalence over vital interpretive nuance.

Moreover, the very act of comparison can be politically charged. When international organizations rank countries by their tax gaps, they may implicitly endorse certain models of governance and fiscal virtue. But what if these rankings obscure more than they reveal? What if they reinforce a technocratic view of compliance that marginalizes local knowledge and alternative fiscal imaginaries?

There is also the issue of administrative and data asymmetries. As already sketched in Section 3.3, the increasing adoption of digital technologies and data-driven enforcement tools by tax administrations has made the capacity to measure and detect evasion increasingly uneven across jurisdictions. Jurisdictions with advanced administrative infrastructures can rely on real-time analytics and integrated reporting systems to produce more granular estimates, whereas lower-capacity administrations often remain dependent on aggregate proxies and limited datasets. As emphasized by Baer et al. (2025), differences in tax administration performance and technological capacity may contribute to significant asymmetries in domestic revenue mobilization and enforcement effectiveness.

Finally, we must consider the political economy of compliance. Tax systems are rarely neutral instruments; they also reflect broader institutional structures and distributions of power within society. As Bird and Martinez-Vazquez (2014) emphasize, tax policy is deeply influenced by institutional legacies, administrative capacity, and political incentives, particularly in developing and transitional economies. Comparative studies that ignore these dynamics risk mistaking symptoms for causes.

Considering these reflections, the goal of comparative research should not be to pursue standardization in isolation, but rather to harmonize formal modeling with institutional contextualization. While analytical frameworks and standardized models are indispensable for identifying core strategic incentives and behavioral regularities, they must be paired with an understanding of how evasion is historically understood, contested, and governed within specific jurisdictions. The ultimate objective is to treat tax evasion not merely as an isolated fiscal puzzle to be solved through uniform technical metrics, but as a dynamic phenomenon that offers a vital window into the broader political economy of the state.

3.5.2 *Case Study: Greece and the Crisis of Fiscal Legitimacy*

Greece offers a compelling illustration of how tax evasion is embedded in broader institutional and cultural dynamics. Prior to the 2008 financial crisis, tax evasion in Greece was widespread but often socially tolerated in certain sectors, framed as a coping mechanism in a system perceived as inefficient and clientelist. The state itself was seen as a poor steward of public resources, and compliance was low not because of weak enforcement alone, but because of a deeper crisis of legitimacy.

During the crisis, however, the narrative has shifted dramatically. Under pressure from international lenders and EU institutions, Greece undertook major fiscal and tax reforms as part of a broader consolidation process (Leventi and Picos Sanchez 2019). The rhetoric around tax evasion changed from a tolerated norm to a moral and civic failure. Campaigns emphasized the link between evasion and austerity, arguing that noncompliance undermined national recovery.

Yet, despite these efforts, compliance gains remained highly uneven across different sectors of the economy. While digital tracking and automated enforcement contributed to reductions in the VAT gap in the subsequent years, structural noncompliance proved stubborn where institutional trust was historically depleted. Indeed, the foundational work by Artavanis et al. (2016) provides an empirical baseline for this resistance: analyzing credit-application data from the pre-crisis period, they demonstrated that tax evasion was overwhelmingly concentrated among self-employed professionals and small businesses. The Greek experience thus highlights the potential limits of technical fixes; when implemented in the absence of a broader political and cultural transformation, such measures fail to rebuild baseline fiscal legitimacy and can instead reinforce low-compliance equilibria. It also underscores the danger of externalized metrics: international comparisons that fail to account for local histories and meanings may misdiagnose the problem, and worse, prescribe solutions that deepen social fragmentation.

3.6 Policy Use of Imperfect Measures

The methodological and comparative challenges discussed in the previous sections do not render tax evasion estimates irrelevant for policymaking. On the contrary, despite their conceptual ambiguities and empirical limitations, these measures continue to play a central role in contemporary fiscal governance. Tax gap estimates and related indicators shape enforcement priorities, guide institutional reforms, influence political narratives, and affect the allocation of administrative resources. The crucial question, therefore, is not whether imperfect measures should be used, but rather how they should be interpreted and operationalized within complex institutional environments.

From this perspective, tax evasion estimates are not merely statistical outputs; they are governance instruments. Their significance lies not only in their numerical precision, but also in their capacity to translate uncertainty into strategic action and approximation into policy design. The following sections examine how these measures influence policy design and enforcement strategies, the risks associated with their misuse, and the potential contribution of interdisciplinary approaches to more adaptive and ethically grounded forms of tax governance.

3.6.1 From Diagnosis to Design: The Strategic Role of Tax Gap Estimates

As discussed in Section 3.2.1, the tax gap serves as the most widely used proxy for tax evasion, despite its conceptual and methodological limitations. In this section, I move from its definitional role to its strategic application, examining how tax gap estimates influence policy design, resource allocation, and enforcement priorities.

The tax gap, that is the difference between taxes owed and taxes paid, is now a central metric in fiscal planning. In the United States, the IRS uses tax gap projections to justify budget allocations, calibrate audit strategies, and advocate for legislative reforms (McDermott 2023).

In the UK, HMRC's annual *Measuring Tax Gaps* reports provide information that supports compliance, analysis and enforcement strategies. In Australia, tax gap estimates and corporate tax transparency initiatives similarly contribute to the broader assessment of tax compliance and fiscal transparency.

These examples show how tax gap estimates can be used not only to allocate resources but also to shape narratives, mobilize political support, and drive innovation in enforcement.

Measurement techniques do more than inform enforcement; they shape the normative architecture of the tax system. When tax gap estimates are used to justify policy decisions, they contribute to defining acceptable behavior and who is deemed noncompliant. This framing influences public discourse, media narratives, and political priorities. As such, the choice of measurement methodology must be guided not only by technical robustness but also by considerations of fairness, transparency, and democratic accountability.

3.6.2 Risks of Misuse: When Numbers Mislead

Yet the power of tax evasion metrics comes with risks. Misinterpreting or misusing these estimates can lead to policy overreach, misallocation of resources, or erosion of taxpayer trust.

One danger is how false precision interacts with distributional insensitivity. Treating tax gap figures as exact, homogeneous metrics can lead to rigid performance targets that distort enforcement priorities.

For example, focusing solely on increasing aggregate audit yields often incentivizes tax authorities to pursue "low-hanging fruit", such as small businesses and self-employed individuals, whose evasion is easier to detect through standard tools. Conversely, this approach neglects complex, sophisticated offshore schemes and legal loopholes concentrated at the top of the income distribution. As argued by Guyton et al. (2023), and consistently with the broader concerns raised by Zucman (2014), when measurement tools understate noncompliance among high-net-worth individuals, enforcement strategies risk becoming regressive, deeply undermining the perceived fairness and systemic legitimacy of the tax institution.

3.6.3 Interdisciplinary Levers for Smarter Policy

To navigate these risks, policymakers must adopt an interdisciplinary approach. More precisely, first, economists provide models of taxpayer behavior and revenue elasticity and legal scholars clarify the boundaries between evasion, avoidance, and error. Then, behavioral scientists design interventions that nudge compliance without coercion. Finally, data scientists develop predictive tools to target enforcement more effectively.

Within this broader interdisciplinary perspective, behavioral approaches have become increasingly relevant in operational tax administration. For example, the World Bank's eMBeD unit has developed the "Behavioral Taxpert's Toolkit", which includes nudges (simplifying forms and personalized reminders), budges (adjusting behavioral incentives and audit perceptions), and trudges (systematically reducing administrative burdens) to improve compliance in different countries across the world.

Globally, randomized field trials and behavioral interventions have shown that relatively simple measures, including targeted reminder letters and behavioral messages, can improve tax compliance, although their effectiveness varies across contexts (Hallsworth et al. 2014; Slemrod 2019).

Legal innovations also matter. The OECD's BEPS framework and Automatic Exchange of Information (AEOI) have transformed the global landscape of tax transparency, enabling countries to detect cross-border evasion and coordinate enforcement (OECD 2015). These initiatives are built on imperfect data, but they have been associated with substantial increases in reported and recovered revenue.

3.6.4 Toward Adaptive and Ethical Tax Governance

The methodological uncertainty surrounding tax evasion estimates has important implications for policy design. Since no measurement technique is fully neutral or bias-free, governments should avoid treating tax gap estimates as precise representations of reality. Instead, tax governance should remain adaptive, transparent, and responsive to changing economic and institutional conditions.

This perspective also highlights the ethical dimension of tax administration. Excessively aggressive enforcement strategies based on uncertain estimates may undermine trust and institutional legitimacy, especially when taxpayers perceive monitoring as arbitrary or disproportionate. Conversely, transparent methodologies, clear communication, and proportional enforcement can strengthen the credibility of tax institutions and improve voluntary compliance over time.

Ultimately, effective tax governance requires balancing measurement, enforcement, and legitimacy. Measurement should therefore support informed and flexible policymaking, rather than creating an illusion of precision that may distort public debate and policy priorities.

3.7 Measuring Beyond the Numbers: A Motivational Approach

Conventional measures of tax evasion, above all the tax gap, are constructed from audit extrapolations, administrative records, and macro-level proxies. Their primary objective is to quantify the magnitude of unpaid liabilities rather than the motivational architecture underlying noncompliance (Slemrod 2007). As a result, traditional measurement approaches tend to focus on observable discrepancies while paying comparatively limited attention to the behavioral and institutional mechanisms that shape compliance decisions.

Over the past two decades, however, behavioral public finance and economic psychology have increasingly demonstrated that compliance cannot be fully explained through deterrence variables alone. Audit probabilities and penalties interact with tax morale, institutional trust, perceived fairness, and social norms in shaping taxpayer behavior. In particular, the psychological tax contract framework and the interaction climate approach emphasize how legitimacy, reciprocity, and respectful treatment may strengthen voluntary cooperation (see Chapter 2). This creates an important methodological tension: while contemporary theories explain compliance through motivational and institutional determinants, most conventional measures of evasion still rely on discrepancy-based metrics that rarely incorporate such dimensions explicitly.

Part of the literature has already moved in the direction of more behaviorally responsive measurement frameworks. Gemmell and Hasseldine (2014), for example, criticize the conventional tax gap as conceptually incomplete because it overlooks taxpayers' behavioral responses to policy and tax administration. Their approach suggests that measurement systems should account not only for unpaid liabilities, but also for how taxpayers adapt to institutional incentives and enforcement environments.

As already mentioned, a parallel development has emerged through simulation-based approaches and agent-based models (ABMs). These models operationalize behavioral and institutional variables within simulated tax systems, incorporating stylized representations of trust, fairness, peer influence, adaptive learning, and norm responsiveness in order to generate aggregate compliance dynamics under different institutional conditions (Hokamp et al. 2018; Vardavas et al. 2019).

Related simulation studies, including econophysics-inspired models based on social interaction structures and public-goods feedback mechanisms, further illustrate how legitimacy and social signals may influence evasion trajectories (Bazart et al. 2016; Hokamp and Seibold 2014).

Collectively, these contributions suggest that motivational and institutional variables are empirically connected to compliance behavior and may therefore play a relevant role in future measurement frameworks.

Operational practice within tax administrations has also increasingly incorporated behavioral insights, such as framing, transparency, simplification, and burden reduction, to improve voluntary compliance, as documented by the OECD's 2021 guidance and the IRS Behavioral Insights Toolkit (OECD 2021). Yet these initiatives primarily influence taxpayer behavior rather than formally redefine official evasion metrics. The tax gap itself remains fundamentally a discrepancy-based measure and is not adjusted through explicit motivational coefficients or institutional trust parameters.

Against this background, the present framework proposes a more integrated interpretative perspective. Rather than relying exclusively on discrepancy-based indicators, traditional tax gap estimates could be complemented by variables related to institutional trust, perceived fairness, civic confidence, and broader compliance attitudes. The underlying idea is that identical levels of measured noncompliance may reflect very different institutional and motivational realities depending on the social context in which they emerge.

From this perspective, tax gap estimates would no longer be interpreted as purely technical and uniform indicators, but as measures embedded within broader institutional and behavioral environments. Such an approach could help tax administrations distinguish more effectively between different underlying drivers of noncompliance, including opportunistic evasion, weak institutional legitimacy, low trust, or widespread perceptions of fiscal unfairness (Luttmer and Singhal 2014; Farrar et al. 2020; Nathan et al. 2026).

This proposal should therefore not be interpreted as a fully operational estimation model, but rather as an exploratory conceptual framework aimed at bridging discrepancy-based measurement with the behavioral and institutional dimensions of compliance. Its objective is not to replace existing tax gap methodologies, but to encourage a broader understanding of how fiscal behavior is shaped within different social and institutional environments.

Rather than offering a definitive solution to the measurement problem, this approach should be understood as a possible direction for future interdisciplinary research combining economics, behavioral science, institutional analysis, and tax administration. Future work may explore how trust indicators, fairness perceptions, and motivational variables could be empirically incorporated into more adaptive compliance metrics capable of capturing not only the magnitude of unpaid liabilities, but also the broader relational health of fiscal systems.

3.8 Conclusion: Measuring the Invisible, Governing Through Approximation

Tax evasion is a phenomenon that resists quantification by its very nature. It thrives in opacity, adapts to enforcement, and evolves with institutional and technological change. Yet, paradoxically, the imperative to measure it remains central to the functioning of modern fiscal states. This chapter has traced the methodological terrain of tax evasion measurement, from conceptual foundations to empirical strategies, from comparative insights to policy applications.

I began by acknowledging the definitional and operational ambiguities that complicate any attempt to pin down what tax evasion is. The tax gap, while widely used, is not a direct measure but a constructed estimate—one that reflects normative assumptions, legal interpretations, and statistical extrapolations. Recognizing these limitations is not a weakness; it is a prerequisite for responsible analysis.

I then explored the methodological challenges inherent in measuring a hidden activity. Selection bias, data scarcity, and model dependence all constrain the reliability of estimates. Yet, through a diverse toolkit, ranging from audit studies and macroeconomic models to machine learning and agent-based simulations, researchers have developed ways to approximate the scale and structure of evasion.

The chapter also examined the comparative dimension, urging caution in cross-country analysis. Tax evasion is embedded in cultural norms, institutional capacities, and political narratives. Comparing tax gaps without accounting for these contextual factors risks misinterpretation and policy misalignment. The case study of Greece illustrated how fiscal legitimacy, public trust, and crisis narratives can reshape both the reality and the perception of evasion.

Perhaps most importantly, I turned to the policy use of imperfect measures, where the stakes are highest. Tax evasion estimates inform budgetary decisions, enforcement strategies, and legal reforms. They guide resource allocation, shape public discourse, and justify interventions. But they can also mislead if treated as precise, if politicized, or if used to target the wrong populations. The challenge is to govern through approximation, not despite it.

This requires a multidisciplinary approach. Economists, legal scholars, behavioral scientists, and data analysts must collaborate to ensure that measurement is not only technically sound but also normatively grounded and socially responsive. It also demands institutional humility: a willingness to revise methods, to communicate uncertainty, and to engage with the public in shaping the meaning and use of tax data.

In revisiting the analytical path traced at the outset (why measurement matters, why it is inherently imperfect, and why acknowledging its limitations is vital) I find that each question remains open-ended, inviting further inquiry rather than closure. The journey through this chapter has shown that measuring tax evasion is not a quest for precision, but for plausibility, a methodological stance that demands both rigor and humility.

The road ahead is both promising and fraught. Advances in data science, international cooperation, and behavioral policy offer new tools for understanding and addressing evasion. But they also raise new questions about privacy, fairness, and the limits of quantification. As we move forward, we must remember that measuring tax evasion is not an end. It is a means to a broader goal: building tax systems that are not only efficient and effective, but also just, transparent, and democratically legitimate.

References

Aliprandi, G. & von Zedlitz, G. (2023). Benchmarking Country-by-Country Reports. EU Tax Observatory Working Paper No. 17. https://doi.org/10.2139/ssrn.4445272

Antinyan, A. & Asatryan, Z. (2025). Nudging for Tax Compliance: A Meta-Analysis. *The Economic Journal* 135(668), 1033–1068.

Artavanis, N., Morse, A. & Tsoutsoura, M. (2016). Measuring Income Tax Evasion Using Bank Credit: Evidence from Greece. *Quarterly Journal of Economics 131* (2), 739–798.

Baer, K., Barra, P. & Benítez, J. C. (2025). Closing the Gap: How Tax Administration Performance Shapes Compliance. IMF Working Paper No. 2025/209 International Monetary Fund, Washington, DC. https://doi.org/10.5089/9798229027076.001

Barra, P., Hutton, E. & Prokofyeva, P. (2023). Corporate Income Tax Gap Estimation by Using Bottom-Up Techniques *in Selected Countries.* IMF Technical Notes and Manuals 2023/06. International Monetary Fund, Washington, DC. https://doi.org/10.5089/9798400246265.005

Bazart, C., Bonein, A., Hokamp, S. & Seibold, G. (2016). Behavioural Economics and Tax Evasion: Calibrating an Agent-Based Econophysics Model with experimental tax compliance data. *Journal of Tax Administration 2*(1), 126–144.

Bird, R. M., & Martinez-Vazquez, J. (2014). *Taxation and Development: The Weakest Link Essays in Honor of Roy Bahl*, Edward Elgar.

Castagna, S. (2023). Comparing Comparability: A Study of EU, ISDS, and WTO Tax 'Like' Cases. *Intertax*, 51(6/7), 487–505.

Cobham, A. & Janský, P. (2018). Global Distribution of Revenue Loss from Corporate Tax Avoidance: Re-Estimation and Country Results. *Journal of International Development* 30(2), 206–232.

EU Tax Observatory. (2025). *Annual Report and Research Outputs.* https://www.taxobservatory.eu

Farrar, J., Massey, D. W., Osecki, E. & Thorne, L. (2020). Tax Fairness: Conceptual Foundations and Empirical Measurement. *Journal of Business Ethics* 162, 487–503.

Feinstein, J. S. (1991). An Econometric Analysis of Income Tax Evasion and Its Detection. *RAND Journal of Economics* 22(1) 14–35.

Gemmell, N. & Hasseldine, J. (2014). Taxpayers' Behavioural Responses and Measures of Tax Compliance "Gaps": A Critique and a New Measure. *Fiscal Studies 35*(3), 275–296.

Guyton, J., Langetieg, P., Reck, D., Risch, M. & Zucman, G. (2023). Tax Evasion at the Top of the Income Distribution: Theory and Evidence, NBER Working Paper 28542. National Bureau of Economic Research, Cambridge, MA. https://doi.org/10.3386/w28542

Hallsworth, M., List, J. A., Metcalfe, R. D. & Vlaev, I. (2014). The Behavioralist as Tax Collector: Using Natural Field Experiments to Enhance Tax Compliance. *Journal of Public Economics* 117, 14–31.

HM Revenue and Customs (2025). *Measuring Tax gaps: Methodological Annex*. GOV.UK.

Hokamp, S., Gulyás, L., Koehler, M. & Wijesinghe, S. (2018). *Agent-Based Modeling and Tax Evasion: Theory and Application*. Wiley Online Library.

Hokamp, S. & Seibold, G. (2014). Tax Compliance and Public Goods Provision: An Agent-Based Econophysics Approach. *Central European Journal of Economic Modelling and Econometrics 6*(4), 217–236.

Leventi, C. & Picos Sanchez, F. (2019). The Tax Structure of an Economy in Crisis: Greece 2009-2017, *JRC Working Papers on Taxation and Structural Reforms, No. 03/2019*, European Commission, Joint Research Centre (JRC), Seville.

Luttmer, E. F. P. & Singhal, M. (2014). Tax Morale. *Journal of Economic Perspectives 28*(4), 149–168.

McDermott, B. (2023, November 30). Unpaid federal taxes and the federal tax gap: Overview, analysis, and policy options. Congressional Research Service, R47858.

Nathan, B. C., Perez-Truglia, R. & Zentner, A. (forthcoming). Paying Your Rair Share: Perceived Fairness and Tax Compliance. *Journal of Accounting and Economics, 81*(2), 101838. https://doi.org/10.1016/j.jacceco.2025.101838

OECD. (2015). *Base Erosion and Profit Shifting (BEPS) Action Plan*. OECD Publishing.

OECD. (2017). *Shining Light on the Shadow Economy: Opportunities and Threats*. OECD Publishing.

OECD. (2021). *International Tax Avoidance and Evasion*. OECD Publishing.

Richupan, S. (1984). *Measuring Tax Evasion: An Introduction to Measurement Techniques. Finance and Development*, IMF.

Schneider, F., & Enste, D. (2000). Shadow Economies: Size, Causes, and Consequences. *Journal of Economic Literature* 38(1), 77–114.

Slemrod, J. (2007). Cheating Ourselves: The Economics of Tax Evasion. *Journal of Economic Perspectives* 21(1), 25–48.

Slemrod, J. (2019). Tax Compliance and Enforcement. *Journal of Economic Literature* 57(4), 904–954.

Tanzi, V. (1983). The Underground Economy in the United States: Estimates and Implications. *IMF Staff Papers* 30(2), 283–305.

Tognato, C. (2015). Narratives of Tax Evasion: The Cultural Legitimacy of Harmful Behavior. In Presser, L., Sandberg, S. (Eds.), *Narrative Criminology*. NYU Press.

van Liebergen, B. (2017). "Machine Learning: A Revolution in Risk-Management and Compliance?" *Journal of Financial Transformation* 45, 60–67.

Vardavas, R., Katkar, P., Parker, A. M., Aliyev, G. R., Graf, M. & Kumar, K. B. (2019). *Agent-Based Model of Income Tax Evasion*. RAND Corporation.

Wintrobe, R., & Gërxhani, K. (2004). Tax Evasion and Trust: A Comparative Analysis. *Proceedings of the Annual Meeting of the European Public Choice Society* (EPCS), Berlin, Germany.

Zucman, G. (2014). Taxing Across Borders: Tracking Personal Wealth and Corporate Profits. *Journal of Economic Perspectives* 28(4), 121–148.

CHAPTER 4

A Simple Theoretical Model

Abstract The last chapter develops a stylized game-theoretic model of tax compliance focused on the strategic interaction between taxpayers and governments. Unlike traditional deterrence models centered mainly on audits and sanctions, the framework emphasizes the joint role of enforcement effectiveness, public expenditure quality, transparency, and taxpayer expectations.

The model identifies multiple equilibrium configurations, including deterrence-based compliance, low-trust evasion, and mixed-strategy equilibria in which taxpayers monitor public good quality with positive probability and the Government provides high-quality goods with positive probability. The analysis highlights how different combinations of enforcement, institutional credibility, and informational conditions may generate markedly different compliance outcomes.

The chapter also discusses the institutional and policy implications of the model and uses comparative examples as stylized reference points for interpreting heterogeneous fiscal environments. More broadly, the chapter proposes interpreting tax compliance not merely as a mechanical response to sanctions, but as the outcome of a strategic and institutional relationship between taxpayers and governments.

Keywords Game theory • Strategic interaction • Equilibrium configurations • Policy design

E. D'Agostino, *The Determinants of Tax Evasion*, Palgrave Studies in Institutions, Economics and Law,
https://doi.org/10.1007/978-3-032-21897-1_4

4.1 From Multidimensional Diagnosis to Strategic Modeling

The previous chapters have shown that tax compliance cannot be interpreted exclusively through deterrence mechanisms or purely financial incentives. Compliance behavior is shaped by a broader set of institutional, psychological, and strategic factors, including trust in public institutions, perceptions of fairness, reciprocity, civic norms, and the perceived quality of public expenditure. At the same time, governments operate under informational and political constraints that affect both enforcement strategies and the credibility of fiscal institutions.

These considerations suggest that tax compliance should be analyzed not simply as an individual decision, but as the outcome of a strategic interaction between taxpayers and the state. Taxpayers decide whether to comply not only because of expected sanctions, but also according to their expectations regarding institutional behavior, public expenditure quality, and the conduct of other taxpayers. Similarly, governments must choose enforcement intensity and expenditure policies while anticipating how taxpayers may respond to different institutional environments.

It is important to clarify that the framework does not explicitly incorporate certain motivational dimensions emphasized in the behavioral literature, such as intrinsic fairness concerns or autonomous ethical preferences. Instead, public expenditure quality is treated as the primary source of perceived reciprocity within the fiscal exchange between taxpayers and the state.

The model could naturally be extended to include heterogeneous taxpayer types, such as individuals who always comply because of strong tax morale or, conversely, taxpayers who always evade regardless of institutional conditions. However, these extreme profiles would add little to the strategic structure of the equilibria, since their behavior would remain fixed independently of enforcement or expenditure quality.

The analysis therefore concentrates on the intermediate category of "conditional" taxpayers whose compliance decisions depend on institutional credibility, enforcement effectiveness, and perceptions of the fiscal exchange. It is precisely these taxpayers who determine the stability or fragility of compliance equilibria and make the interaction between taxation, enforcement, and public goods quality strategically relevant. Within this framework, informational asymmetries are treated strictly as strategic constraints under which these taxpayers imperfectly observe actual government behavior, leaving the historical and empirical validation of these specific parameters to the comparative reference points developed in the subsequent sections.

By focusing on these dimensions, the framework preserves analytical tractability while remaining connected to the broader behavioral and institutional insights developed throughout the book.

The equilibrium analysis developed in the following sections shows how different institutional conditions may generate markedly different compliance outcomes. In some environments, cooperation and voluntary compliance may emerge as stable outcomes sustained by credible institutions and effective enforcement. In others, weak institutional credibility and limited monitoring may instead favor persistent evasion and unstable fiscal equilibria.

The remainder of the chapter develops the analytical framework progressively, moving from the conceptual foundations of the interaction between taxpayers and the government to its formal representation and institutional implications. After introducing the strategic logic underlying tax compliance decisions, the chapter presents the structure of the model and discusses the equilibrium configurations that emerge under different institutional settings. Particular attention is devoted to the policy implications of the framework and to the way alternative institutional environments may shape compliance incentives across countries. The chapter concludes by reflecting on the broader implications and limitations of the proposed model.

4.2 Strategic Interaction and the Logic of Compliance

The model presented here aims to shed light on the interaction between external incentives and institutional reciprocity by investigating how the level of tax enforcement affects the relationship between tax compliance and the quality of public expenditure provided. To examine this dynamic, this section formalizes the rules of the game and the strategic choices available to each player. The game involves two principal actors: the government and a single taxpayer.

The government sets a fiscal policy vector consisting of the tax rate, the quality of public expenditure (either high or low), and the intensity or probability of tax enforcement, whereas the taxpayer decides whether to pay/evade taxes after he observes both the tax rate and the enforcement level, but not the quality of expenditure (unless he pays a monitoring cost).

These choices are interdependent. For example, increasing enforcement may boost compliance in the short term, but if it undermines trust, it may reduce voluntary compliance over time. Similarly, improving the quality of public services may enhance legitimacy and reduce the need for coercion, but requires sufficient revenue and institutional capacity.

The model assumes that high-quality expenditure is more expensive to produce than low-quality spending, but more valuable from a taxpayer's perspective. Further, investing in law enforcement is costly for the government, but it allows to detect evasion with positive probability; conversely, if no enforcement is implemented, the decision of paying/evading taxes is left to the taxpayer's satisfaction about the (expected) quality of public expenditure compared to the tax rate requested.

What makes this interaction a strategic game is the fact that each player's optimal strategy depends on expectations regarding the behavior of the other player. Taxpayers evaluate not only the probability of enforcement and sanctions, but also the expected quality of public expenditure and the informational cost associated with verifying it. The government, in turn, anticipates how taxpayers will react to different combinations of taxation, enforcement, and expenditure quality.

This mutual anticipation generates strategic feedback effects. When enforcement is sufficiently effective and public expenditure is perceived as credible, taxpayers are more likely to comply, thereby stabilizing the fiscal system and reducing incentives toward opportunistic behavior. Conversely, when expenditure quality is perceived as low and institutional credibility weakens, taxpayers may increasingly view evasion as individually rational, especially if enforcement is ineffective or informational asymmetries remain high.

The government must therefore balance deterrence and legitimacy, recognizing that compliance is not imposed, but rather earned. This perspective aligns with the Slippery Slope Framework (Kirchler et al. 2008), which argues that compliance is shaped by both enforcement power and institutional trust (see Section 2.4.3). The fiscal contract between state and citizen is sustained not only by the threat of punishment, but also by the perception of fairness, reciprocity, and shared purpose.

The next section presents a formal model that captures these dynamics, offering a structured framework for analyzing how enforcement, legitimacy, and taxpayer behavior interact to shape compliance outcomes.

4.3 Formalizing the Model

I now present a stylized game-theoretic model that formalizes the strategic interaction between taxpayers and the government. The model is intentionally simple, designed to capture the essential trade-offs that shape compliance behavior.

The game consists of three stages and is played by the (G)overnment and a single (T)axpayer.

In stage 1 G sets the policy $\{t, q, e\}$, where:

- $t \leq t_{max}$ is the tax rate;
- $q = (l, h)$ is the quality of public expenditure. To simplify, we say it can be either (l)ow or (h)igh;
- $e = \{0, \bar{e}\}$ is the tax enforcement policy, that could be either implemented to detect T's misbehavior with probability $w > 0$ (if $e = \bar{e}$) or not implemented (if $e = 0$).

Producing quality q c_q $c_h > c_l > 0$ $e = \bar{e}$ $k > 0$, which will be transferred to T $e = 0$.

In stage 2 T observes t and e $m > 0$ to observe q. T's evaluation for q $u_q Y$ $u_h = t_{max} > u_l > 0$, and income Y is normalized to 1. Then, a strategy for T specifies whether he pays/evades t and whether he monitors q, including his decision after monitoring.

In stage 3 G implements her policy and T discovers the quality of public expenditure, if not already monitored.

G's payoff corresponds to the tax revenue minus any cost incurred (precisely, c_q and eventually k). T's payoff is his evaluation minus the tax rate paid (eventually including the fine if caught to be evader) and, eventually, the monitoring cost. If T evades and is not prosecuted, G has no revenue to finance public expenditure: both players earn 0.

Throughout the chapter we assume that $u_h - c_h - m - k > 0 > u_l - c_l$, meaning that it is always (resp. never) socially efficient that G provides high-quality (resp. low-quality) expenditure.

I solve the game by searching for Perfect Bayesian equilibria in pure and mixed strategies, where T's belief assigns a probability distribution over quality, given t and e: for every $t \leq u_h$ $e = \{0, \bar{e}\}$. Given the large variety of PBEs, I use a restriction on out-of-equilibrium beliefs such that if T observes G deviating from the policy the equilibrium prescribes, then T

attaches probability 1 that the deviating policy includes low-quality expenditure. Then, I select only those equilibria with enforcement in order to isolate its effect on the relevant parameters.

4.4 Equilibrium Logic and Strategic Configurations

4.4.1 *Introduction*

The model admits multiple equilibrium configurations depending on enforcement effectiveness, public expenditure quality, institutional credibility, and taxpayers' monitoring capacity.

First, the game may generate a deterrence-based compliance equilibrium in which the government adopts high enforcement and provides public expenditure of low quality, while taxpayers choose to comply. In this configuration, voluntary cooperation is sustained by the expected cost of evasion generated by enforcement. Social welfare remains negative because low-quality expenditure is socially inefficient.

Second, the model may generate a low-trust evasion equilibrium characterized by weak institutional credibility, low-quality public expenditure, and ineffective enforcement. In this case, taxpayers strategically choose evasion, despite the government implementing enforcement. Social welfare is comparatively low due to persistent noncompliance, fragile reciprocal expectations, and reduced institutional legitimacy.

Finally, the model also admits mixed-strategy equilibria in which both taxpayers and governments randomize their strategies. In these configurations, compliance and public expenditure quality become unstable and highly sensitive to expectations, informational asymmetries, and monitoring conditions. Social welfare assumes intermediate values and may fluctuate according to institutional credibility and taxpayers' beliefs regarding governmental behavior.

The following sections formally present the model and analyze each equilibrium configuration in greater detail, emphasizing both its strategic foundations and its institutional interpretation.

4.4.2 *Deterrence-Based Compliance Equilibrium*

The first equilibrium identified by the model can be defined as a Deterrence-Based Compliance Equilibrium. In this configuration, the Government implements tax enforcement, provides low-quality public expenditure, and sets a relatively moderate tax rate, $t^* = u_l + \frac{wk}{1-w}$, while taxpayers choose to pay taxes without monitoring the quality of public expenditure. Formally, the equilibrium strategy profile is therefore characterized by $\{t^*, l, \bar{e}\}$, with taxpayers complying directly rather than incurring the monitoring cost necessary to verify expenditure quality.

The intuition behind this equilibrium is closely related to the classical deterrence framework introduced by Allingham and Sandmo (1972). When the probability of detection is sufficiently high, evasion becomes excessively risky relative to compliance. Taxpayers therefore prefer to pay taxes even though the quality of public expenditure remains low. Compliance is not generated by institutional trust, reciprocity, or civic identification with the fiscal system, but primarily by the expected cost associated with sanctions and enforcement.

In the present equilibrium, taxpayers comply because enforcement is effective, not because taxation is perceived as fair or because public expenditure is viewed as particularly valuable. Since taxpayers do not monitor expenditure quality in equilibrium, the government has no incentive to provide high-quality public goods and optimally selects the low-quality option.

This result highlights an important asymmetry between compliance and institutional legitimacy. A government may succeed in stabilizing tax compliance through credible enforcement while simultaneously failing to generate strong reciprocal expectations between taxpayers and public institutions. In this sense, the equilibrium captures fiscal systems in which administrative capacity is sufficiently developed to sustain compliance, but public expenditure quality and institutional credibility remain relatively weak.

The equilibrium is therefore consistent with institutional environments in which deterrence plays the dominant role in sustaining fiscal order. In such contexts, taxpayers comply primarily because evasion is costly, while the fiscal exchange itself remains only weakly cooperative. The model suggests that this type of equilibrium may be relatively stable as long as enforcement remains sufficiently effective. If enforcement effectiveness declines, taxpayers have little intrinsic motivation to continue complying, and incentives toward evasion may rapidly re-emerge.

From a welfare perspective, the equilibrium is not optimal. Although tax compliance is achieved, the government provides low-quality expenditure, implying that enforcement alone is insufficient to guarantee socially efficient fiscal outcomes. The equilibrium therefore illustrates one of the central implications of the model: effective deterrence can sustain compliance, but it does not necessarily produce high-quality public expenditure, institutional legitimacy, or durable cooperative fiscal relations.

4.4.3 *Low-Trust Evasion Equilibrium*

The second equilibrium identified by the model can be defined as a Low-Trust Evasion Equilibrium. In this configuration, the government implements tax enforcement and sets the highest available tax rate together with low-quality public expenditure, formally $\{t_{max}, l, \bar{e}\}$, while taxpayers choose to evade taxes without monitoring expenditure quality.

Unlike the previous equilibrium, enforcement is not sufficiently effective to induce compliance, and taxpayers therefore regard evasion as the individually rational strategy.

The logic underlying this equilibrium is fundamentally different from the deterrence-based configuration discussed above. Here, the probability of detection is too low to offset the perceived burden of taxation. Since public expenditure quality is low and taxpayers do not expect a sufficiently valuable fiscal return, compliance loses its attractiveness and evasion emerges as the equilibrium outcome.

The equilibrium remains broadly consistent with the classical economic intuition developed by Allingham and Sandmo (1972). However, the model also highlights a more institutional dimension of tax compliance. The problem is not simply that enforcement is weak, but that the overall fiscal exchange is perceived as unfavorable. High taxation combined with low-quality expenditure undermines reciprocal expectations between taxpayers and the state, weakening the incentives to comply voluntarily.

This equilibrium therefore captures institutional environments characterized by fragile legitimacy, limited fiscal reciprocity, and persistent skepticism toward public institutions. In such contexts, governments may rely formally on enforcement and taxation yet fail to generate widespread compliance because taxpayers perceive public expenditure as ineffective, unfair, or disconnected from their contributions. The resulting fiscal relationship becomes conflictual rather than cooperative, with evasion increasingly normalized as a rational response to institutional inefficiency.

An important implication of the equilibrium is that stronger taxation alone cannot guarantee higher compliance. When enforcement effectiveness remains limited and expenditure quality is perceived as poor, increasing the tax burden may instead intensify incentives toward evasion. The equilibrium thus illustrates how weak institutional credibility can transform taxation into a destabilizing source of fiscal conflict.

From a welfare perspective, this is the most problematic equilibrium generated by the model. Taxpayers evade, public expenditure quality remains low, and enforcement fails to restore cooperative behavior. The fiscal system therefore enters a low-compliance trap in which weak institutional legitimacy, ineffective enforcement, and opportunistic expectations reinforce one another.

4.4.4 Conditional Cooperation Mixed Equilibria

Beyond the pure-strategy equilibria discussed above, the model also generates a class of mixed-strategy equilibria. In these equilibria, the government randomizes between low- and high-quality public expenditure, while taxpayers randomize between paying taxes directly and monitoring expenditure quality. Formally, the government mixes between $\{t, l, \bar{e}\}$ and $\{t, h, \bar{e}\}$, with intermediate values of t, whereas taxpayers mix between monitoring (and paying only when high-quality expenditure is observed) and paying without monitoring.

These equilibria arise only under specific informational conditions. In particular, monitoring must be sufficiently cheap for taxpayers to consider verifying the quality of public expenditure. If monitoring is too costly, taxpayers will not acquire information, and the government has no incentive to provide high-quality expenditure. Conversely, when monitoring is cheap enough, taxpayers can discipline government behavior by conditioning compliance on the observed quality of public spending. The possibility of monitoring therefore gives public expenditure quality strategic relevance.

The intuition behind this result is that compliance is no longer sustained by deterrence alone. Taxpayers are willing to pay only when they attach sufficient value to the fiscal exchange and when they can verify, at reasonable cost, whether the government provides high-quality expenditure. At the same time, the government is willing to provide high-quality expenditure with positive probability because doing so can induce taxpayers to comply. The equilibrium is therefore based on conditional cooperation: taxpayers do not trust the government unconditionally, but they may comply when credible information about public expenditure quality becomes available.

This result highlights an informational dimension that is often implicit in behavioral accounts of fiscal legitimacy. Taxpayers do not respond only to audit probabilities and sanctions; they also respond to the perceived credibility of the tax–public goods exchange. When this credibility is uncertain, monitoring and transparency become central to the sustainability of compliance.

The mixed-strategy equilibria are therefore especially relevant for understanding intermediate fiscal environments. They do not describe a fully cooperative regime, in which compliance is sustained by stable trust, nor a purely deterrence-based regime, in which compliance depends almost exclusively on enforcement. Rather, they capture a transitional configuration in which taxpayers' willingness to comply depends on whether public expenditure quality is observable, credible, and sufficiently valuable.

From a policy perspective, the key implication is that transparency can change the strategic structure of compliance. By reducing the cost of monitoring public expenditure and making the use of tax revenues more visible, governments can strengthen the conditions under which taxpayers are willing to comply. In this sense, tools such as transparent budgeting, public expenditure dashboards, participatory budgeting, and clear communication about service delivery may shift the system away from fragile conditional compliance and toward more stable cooperative patterns.

4.5 Comparative Institutional Configurations

One of the purposes of any formal model is to provide a simplified analytical structure capable of capturing recurring mechanisms observable in reality. At the same time, actual tax systems are shaped by historical legacies, political dynamics, cultural norms, administrative capacities, and institutional complexities that cannot be fully reproduced within a stylized game-theoretic framework. For this reason, the equilibria generated by the model should not be interpreted as rigid classifications of existing countries. Rather, they provide stylized institutional benchmarks that help identify how different combinations of enforcement effectiveness, public expenditure quality, transparency, and taxpayer expectations may influence compliance behavior across heterogeneous institutional environments.

A first broad category includes enforcement-dominated institutional environments in which tax compliance is sustained primarily through credible deterrence mechanisms despite relatively weak perceptions regarding the quality of public expenditure or the reciprocity of the fiscal exchange. In these contexts, administrative capacity and enforcement effectiveness therefore become the principal foundations of fiscal stability. These environments are broadly compatible with the Deterrence-Based Compliance Equilibrium generated by the model.

Although no real-world fiscal system perfectly corresponds to this equilibrium, some highly enforcement-oriented institutional environments may display features broadly consistent with its logic. Certain aspects of the Singaporean fiscal system, for example, are often associated with strong administrative capacity, effective enforcement, and limited tolerance toward noncompliance. This example should therefore be interpreted only as an illustrative approximation of some characteristics associated with deterrence-based compliance rather than as a complete representation of the equilibrium itself.

A second broad category includes low-trust institutional environments characterized by weak institutional credibility, unstable public expenditure quality, limited transparency, and high perceived corruption. Weak reciprocal expectations and persistent skepticism toward public institutions therefore reinforce incentives toward evasion and undermine voluntary compliance. These environments are broadly compatible with the Low-Trust Evasion Equilibrium generated by the model.

Greece during the sovereign debt crisis may illustrate some features broadly consistent with this equilibrium. High fiscal pressure, declining institutional trust, and widespread perceptions of inefficiency and unfairness contributed to weakening cooperative compliance incentives and increasing tolerance toward evasion (Artavanis et al. 2016; Leventi and Picos 2019). Similar mechanisms are discussed in the literature on corruption, administrative fragmentation, and informal economies (Mauro 1995; Schneider and Enste 2000; Medina and Schneider 2018).

Between these two polar configurations lie a broader set of intermediate institutional environments broadly compatible with the Conditional Cooperation Mixed Equilibria generated by the model. In these contexts, compliance is neither sustained exclusively by deterrence nor supported by fully internalized institutional trust. Rather, taxpayers' willingness to comply depends on whether public expenditure is perceived as sufficiently credible, observable, and reciprocally valuable.

A first variant includes relatively transparent and administratively coordinated environments in which taxpayers maintain reasonably stable expectations regarding institutional performance. Here, monitoring costs are relatively low, administrative information is accessible, and enforcement operates alongside institutional credibility rather than replacing it entirely. Countries such as Germany or the Netherlands may illustrate some features of this configuration, where compliance is supported by a combination of enforcement, transparency, and predictable public administration.

A second variant emerges in more fragmented institutional environments which may remain compatible with forms of conditional cooperation, although under significantly more unstable conditions. Here, perceptions regarding institutional quality and reciprocal fairness vary across regions, sectors, or social groups, making compliance highly contingent on taxpayers' expectations about both governmental behavior and the conduct of others. Italy, particularly in the presence of strong regional asymmetries and heterogeneous levels of civic capital, may illustrate some aspects of this more fragile and fragmented version of conditional cooperation (Putnam 1993; D'Agostino et al. 2021).

Since the model does not include explicit parameters related to fairness, tax morale, and intrinsic motivations, there are also institutional environments that it cannot fully capture. This is the case of exceptionally high-trust cooperative contexts, where compliance appears to be sustained not only by institutional credibility and administrative effectiveness, but also by deeply internalized norms of fairness, civic reciprocity, and social cooperation. This interpretation is broadly consistent with the literature on quality of government and institutional trust developed by Rothstein (2011), Kumlin and Rothstein (2005), and Svallfors (2013). Scandinavian countries are often discussed in the literature as approximate examples of this broader institutional environment.

However, this limitation is itself theoretically informative as it indirectly reinforces one of the broader arguments developed throughout the book: when motivational and cultural dimensions become sufficiently strong within a society, they may sustain stable compliance patterns that extend beyond the strategic incentives and informational mechanisms formalized in standard deterrence-based frameworks.

4.6 Concluding Remarks

This chapter has developed a stylized game-theoretic model of tax compliance between taxpayers and the government. Building on the interdisciplinary perspectives discussed throughout the book, the analysis has shown how compliance depends not only on enforcement intensity, but also on public expenditure quality, institutional credibility, monitoring conditions, and taxpayers' expectations regarding the fiscal exchange.

Consequently, the model operates not as a deterministic classification tool, but as a stylized analytical tool for interpreting heterogeneous institutional environments. As demonstrated by the international cases examined in this chapter, real-world fiscal dynamics reflect hybrid features shaped by political instability, administrative capacity, cultural norms, and historical legacies that continuously interact with the core strategic incentives identified by the framework.

The chapter has also emphasized the importance of informational dimensions in tax compliance. Taxpayers do not observe public expenditure perfectly, nor can they always evaluate the true quality of public goods and institutional performance. As a result, transparency, visibility, and monitoring become central elements in sustaining credible fiscal relations and stable compliance expectations. In this respect, the model reinforces one of the broader arguments developed throughout the book: long-term tax compliance depends not only on deterrence, but also on the quality and credibility of the institutional environment in which the fiscal relationship operates.

At the same time, the model intentionally abstracts from several dimensions that are likely to play an important role in real-world fiscal systems. First, taxpayers are assumed to be homogeneous, whereas actual compliance behavior is strongly influenced by differences in income, social norms, political preferences, risk attitudes, and access to information. Introducing heterogeneous taxpayers could generate more complex strategic interactions and multiple forms of conditional compliance.

Second, the model does not explicitly incorporate the role of media, political communication, or information manipulation. In reality, taxpayers' perceptions regarding public expenditure quality are often mediated by political narratives, media framing, and institutional communication strategies. Public visibility and transparency are therefore likely to depend not only on objective expenditure quality, but also on how information is transmitted and interpreted within the public sphere.

Third, governments are modeled primarily as strategic actors maximizing fiscal objectives within the structure of the game. The framework does not distinguish explicitly between governments genuinely oriented toward collective welfare and governments primarily motivated by electoral incentives, political survival, or short-term consensus maximization. Introducing alternative political objectives could significantly alter equilibrium behavior, especially with respect to expenditure quality and transparency decisions.

The model also abstracts from several additional factors that may shape compliance dynamics, including administrative inefficiencies, corruption within tax authorities, macroeconomic instability, informal labor markets, international fiscal constraints, and long-run reputational effects. Moreover, the analysis remains static and therefore cannot fully capture the path-dependent evolution of trust, cooperative expectations, and social norms emphasized in the broader behavioral literature on tax compliance.

These limitations naturally suggest several directions for future research. A dynamic extension of the model could analyze how repeated interactions between taxpayers and governments gradually influence institutional trust and compliance incentives over time. Additional extensions could introduce taxpayer heterogeneity, endogenous political incentives, media influence, or asymmetric information regarding public expenditure quality. It would also be possible to incorporate behavioral elements more explicitly, including bounded rationality, fairness concerns, and evolving social norms.

More broadly, the model developed in this chapter suggests that tax systems should not be interpreted exclusively through deterrence mechanisms. Compliance depends not only on governments' capacity to punish evasion, but also on the broader institutional conditions that shape taxpayers' expectations regarding fairness, public expenditure, and state credibility.

Appendix: Formal Proofs of Model Equilibria

The appendix provides a fully formalized equilibrium derivation for the model presented in Chapoter 4.

$\bar{u} = u_h - u_l$, $\bar{c} = c_h - c_l$ $A = \sqrt{\bar{u}^2 + 4k\left(u_l - c_l\right)}$ and

$$w^* = \min\left\{\frac{t-c_l}{t-c_l+k}, \frac{u_h-c_l+u_l-c_h-\sqrt{(u_h-c_l+u_l-c_h)^2-4\left(u_h+k-c_l\right)\left(u_h-c_h\right)}}{2(u_h+k-c_l}\right\}.$$

Call x the probability of G setting high quality.

Proposition 1

1. If $w > \frac{(u_h+u_l-2c_l)+A}{2(u_h+k-c_l)}$, G sets $\{t^*, l, \bar{e}\}$ where $t^* = u_l + \frac{wk}{1-w}$, and T pays without monitoring in the unique equilibrium: players respectively get $u_l + \frac{wk}{1-w} - c_l - \frac{wk}{1-w}$.
2. If $w < \frac{(u_h+u_l-2c_l)+A}{2(u_h+k-c_l)}$, G sets $\{u_h, l, \bar{e}\}$ and T evades without monitoring: players respectively get $w(u_l + k - c_l) - k$ and $-w(u_h + k - u_l)$.

   This equilibrium is unique if $w \in \left(w^*, \frac{(u_h+u_l-2c_l)+A}{2(u_h+k-c_l)}\right)$ or if the monitoring cost is expensive. Otherwise,
3. There also exists a class of equilibria with G mixing between $\{t, l, \bar{e}\}$ and $\{t, h, \bar{e}\}$, where $t > t^*$, and T mixing between paying taxes and monitoring (paying only if $q = h$ and evading otherwise). Players respectively get $t - c_h - k$ and $x\bar{u} + u_l - t$. Social welfare is positive only if x is large enough.

Proof

No equilibrium exists in which G sets $\{t, h, e\}$, where $e = \{0, \bar{e}\}$:

- G could profitably deviate to $\{t, l, e\}$ to save $\bar{c}$ if T does not monitor;
- T could profitably deviate to not monitoring to save m, otherwise.

No equilibrium exists in which G sets $\{t, l, 0\}$: since $t \geq c_l$, the Efficiency Constraint states that T would evade and G could profitably deviate to $e = \bar{e}$. This said, I can move to the proof of each equilibrium:

1. T cannot profitably deviate to evading because $t = u_l + wk/(1-w)$. G cannot profitably deviate to setting u_h, which T would evade, because $w > \frac{(u_h+u_l-2c_l)+A}{2(u_h+k-c_l)}$.

2. G cannot profitably deviate to another tax rate $t \leq u_l + wk/(1-w)$, which T would fulfill because $w \leq \frac{(u_h+u_l-2c_l)+A}{2(u_h+k-c_l)}$; T cannot deviate to paying if $w \leq \frac{\bar{u}}{(\bar{u}+k)} > \frac{(u_h+u_l-2c_l)+A}{2(u_h+k-c_l)}$.
3. T is indifferent between monitoring and paying iff $t = u_l + \frac{wk}{1-w} + \frac{m}{(1-x)(1-w)}$, with $\frac{\partial t}{\partial w} > 0$ and $\partial t/\partial x > 0$. T does not deviate to evading without monitoring iff

$$x \in \left[\frac{1-Z}{2}, \frac{1+Z}{2}\right] \equiv \left[x_{min}, x_{max}\right],$$

where $Z = \sqrt{1-\frac{4m}{\bar{u}}}$. It requires $m \leq \bar{u}/4$.

Call y the probability of T monitoring. G is indifferent between low and high quality iff

$$y = \frac{\bar{c}}{(t-c_l)(1-w)-wk},$$

which is less than 1 if

$$x > 1-\frac{m}{(1-w)(c_l-u_l)+\bar{c}} \equiv \hat{x}.$$

G cannot profitably deviate to either $\{u_l + wk/(1-w), l, \bar{e}\}$, which T would pay, if

$$x > 1-\frac{m}{(1-w)\bar{c}} < \hat{x},$$

or to $\{u_h, l, \hat{e}\}$, which T would evade, if

$$x > 1 - \frac{m}{(1-w)(u_h-c_l)} - w^2k + (1-w)(c_h-u_l) \equiv 1 - \frac{m}{H}.$$

Therefore $m \leq \min\left\{K\left(1-\frac{K}{\bar{u}}\right), H\left(1-\frac{H}{\bar{u}}\right)\right\}$, where $K = (1-w)(c_l-u_l)+\bar{c}$, this equilibrium exists for $x \in \left[\max\left\{1-\frac{m}{K}, 1-\frac{m}{H}\right\}, x_{max}\right] \equiv \left[x_-, x_{max}\right]$.

Out-of-equilibrium beliefs exclude a profitable deviation to a higher/lower t. Social welfare [viz. $x\bar{u} - (c_h - u_l)$] is positive if $x \in \left[\frac{c_h + k - u_l}{\bar{u}}, x_{max}\right]$.■

References

Allingham, M. G. & Sandmo, A. (1972). Income Tax Evasion: A Theoretical Analysis. *Journal of Public Economics* 1(3–4), 323–338.

Artavanis, N., Morse, A. & Tsoutsoura, M. (2016). Measuring Income Tax Evasion Using Bank Credit: Evidence from Greece. *Quarterly Journal of Economics* 131(2), 739–798.

D'Agostino, E., De Benedetto, M. A. & Sobbrio, G. (2021). Tax Evasion and Government Size: Evidence from Italian Provinces. *Economia Politica* 38(3), 1149–1187.

Kirchler, E., Hoelzl, E. & Wahl, I. (2008). Enforced versus Voluntary Tax Compliance: The "Slippery Slope" Framework. *Journal of Economic Psychology* 29(2), 210–225.

Kumlin, S., & Rothstein, B. (2005). Making and Breaking Social Capital: The Impact of Welfare-State Institutions. *Comparative Political Studies* 38(4), 339–365.

Leventi, C. & Picos Sanchez, F. (2019). The Tax Structure of an Economy in Crisis: Greece 2009-2017, *JRC Working Papers on Taxation and Structural Reforms, No. 03/2019*, European Commission, Joint Research Centre (JRC), Seville.

Mauro, P. (1995). Corruption and Growth. *Quarterly Journal of Economics* 110(3), 681–712.

Medina, L., & Schneider, F. (2018). Shadow Economies around the World: What did we Learn over the Last 20 Years? *IMF Working Paper*, International Monetary Fund, Washington, DC. https://doi.org/10.5089/9781484338636.001

Putnam, R. D. (1993). *Making Democracy Work: Civic Traditions in Modern Italy*. Princeton University Press.

Rothstein, B. (2011). *The Quality of Government: Corruption, Social Trust, and Inequality in International Perspective*. University of Chicago Press.

Schneider, F., & Enste, D. (2000). Shadow Economies: Size, Causes, and Consequences. *Journal of Economic Literature* 38(1), 77–114.

Svallfors, S. (2013). Government Quality, Egalitarianism, and Attitudes to Taxes and Social Spending: A European Comparison. *European Political Science Review* 5(3), 363–380.

Concluding Reflections

Tax evasion is a phenomenon so familiar that it risks being underestimated, and yet so persistent that it demands renewed intellectual and policy attention. It is not just a matter of numbers or norms, but a reflection of how citizens perceive the legitimacy of institutions, the perceived fairness of the fiscal system, and the meaning of civic responsibility. If taxation is the price we pay for civilization, then evasion is its silent protest.

This book has explored the determinants of tax evasion through a multidimensional lens. While the core analytical focus lies in the interplay between extrinsic incentives and intrinsic motivations, as developed in Chapter 2, the phenomenon cannot be fully understood without first deconstructing its broader implications. Chapter 1 offered an interdisciplinary perspective that situates evasion within legal ambiguity, sociological dynamics, political legitimacy, psychological perception, and economic distortion. It argued that tax evasion is not merely a breach of law, but a signal of deeper tensions between state and society.

Chapter 3 addressed the empirical challenge of measuring what is meant to be hidden. How large is the tax gap? Where is evasion concentrated? How does it evolve over time? These questions are not only technical—they are political and normative. Measurement shapes perception, and perception shapes policy. The chapter showed that while no method is perfect, acknowledging uncertainty is essential for designing credible and adaptive strategies.

E. D'Agostino, *The Determinants of Tax Evasion*, Palgrave Studies in Institutions, Economics and Law,
https://doi.org/10.1007/978-3-032-21897-1

Chapter 4 developed a stylized game-theoretic model of tax compliance focused on the strategic interaction between taxpayers and governments. The analysis showed how different institutional configurations may generate markedly different equilibria, ranging from deterrence-based compliance to low-cooperation environments characterized by weak institutional credibility and persistent incentives toward evasion. The model also highlighted the importance of transparency and conditional cooperation, suggesting that stable compliance depends not only on governments' capacity to punish evasion, but also on their ability to sustain stable and credible forms of fiscal cooperation over time.

But why do we study a phenomenon that seems so obvious? Because its persistence is not inevitable. Understanding tax evasion is the first step toward reducing it. Policymakers need more than moral appeals or punitive instruments: they need strategies that work. Acting on external levers such as audits and penalties is effective, but costly. Investing in civic education and normative change is essential, but slow. The solution may lie in a balance: in designing systems that align incentives with values, and that make paying taxes feel less like a burden and more like a contribution.

One promising path is to govern well. When citizens see their taxes transformed into visible, high-quality public services, like clean streets, functioning schools, accessible healthcare, the fiscal exchange becomes tangible. Trust grows, and compliance follows. This is not utopia; it is institutional pragmatism.

Looking ahead, much remains to be done. Future research should explore the behavioral resilience of tax systems: how compliance holds up under stress, and how trust can be rebuilt after it is lost. More work is needed on the digital transformation of taxation, on the role of local governance, and on the ethical design of behavioral interventions. Comparative studies should continue to illuminate how culture, history, and institutional design shape fiscal behavior.

The fight against tax evasion is not only about revenue collection; it also concerns democratic legitimacy and social cohesion. At a time when governments face mounting fiscal pressures, from climate change to demographic shifts, from digitalization to geopolitical uncertainty, the sustainability of public finance depends critically on tax compliance. Evasion undermines not only revenues but also the legitimacy of democratic institutions and the cohesion of societies.

The central message of this book is that compliance is neither purely a matter of fear nor purely a matter of virtue. It is the outcome of a complex interaction between citizens, institutions, and fiscal incentives. Governments that recognize this complexity and invest not only in enforcement capacity but also in institutional credibility and public trust are more likely to secure sustainable, equitable, and efficient tax systems. And while the road is long, the destination is worth pursuing: a society where compliance is not coerced but chosen; where taxation is not feared but understood; and where the fiscal contract is not imposed, but shared.

Index

E. D'Agostino, *The Determinants of Tax Evasion*, Palgrave Studies in Institutions, Economics and Law,
https://doi.org/10.1007/978-3-032-21897-1

Zeitfracht Medien GmbH
Ferdinand-Jühlke-Straße 7
99095 Erfurt, Deutschland
produktsicherheit@kolibri360.de